Fair Housing

Marcia L. Russell, DREI

This publication is designed to provide accurate and authoritative information in regard to the subject matter covered. It is sold with the understanding that the publisher is not engaged in rendering legal, accounting, or other professional advice. If legal advice or other expert assistance is required, the services of a competent professional should be sought.

President: Dr. Andrew Temte
Chief Learning Officer: Dr. Tim Smaby
Vice President, Real Estate Education: Asha Alsobrooks
Development Editor: Jennifer Brandt

FAIR HOUSING FOURTH EDITION

Published by DF Institute, Inc., d/b/a Dearborn Real Estate Education
332 Front St. S., Suite 501
La Crosse, WI 54601

Printed in the United States of America
Second printing 2012
ISBN: 978-1-4277-1156-4 / 1-4277-1156-9
PPN: 2111-1204

contents

Chapter 4

Fair Housing Advertising 46

Chapter 5

Fair Housing Enforcement 58

Chapter 6

Cultural Diversity and Fair Housing 70

Chapter 7

Fair Housing Case Studies 82

introduction

Equal opportunity in housing is still an elusive dream for many people in America. The Housing Discrimination Study conducted by the U.S. Department of Housing and Urban Development (HUD) in 2000 provides strong and very credible evidence that discrimination persists today in urban housing markets nationwide. The study found that African Americans and Hispanics who search for housing or inquire about mortgage financing options are still being denied the information and the opportunities that whites take for granted. The study also found some troubling indications that steering—geographic steering to different kinds of neighborhoods—is on the rise, as is deferential assistance with the mortgage financing process.

The Housing Discrimination Study focused on inquiries about the rental and sale of housing in metropolitan markets nationwide. It found that the overall incidence of discrimination against minority homeseekers ranges from 17 percent for black homebuyers to 26 percent for Hispanic renters. This is an overall summary measure that indicates that in roughly one out of five visits to a real estate or rental office, a minority customer is not going to get as good information, as much information, as much help and assistance as a comparably qualified white customer.

HUD has invested in three roughly decennial studies of housing discrimination nationwide and can measure change over time in levels of discrimination. In 1989, looking at the 1977 to 1989 period, the study found no evidence of any change in the incidence of discrimination nationwide. However, the study of the 1990s, comparing 2000 results with 1989 results, found a significant reduction in discrimination, consistently measured at the two points in time for both black and Hispanic homebuyers and for black renters. Only Hispanic renters appeared to face the same levels of discrimination today that they did in 1989, although this overall pattern is declining, especially on the homeownership side.

Today's real estate practitioner must establish business practices that comply with fair housing laws and offer equal professional service to all. Consistency, objectivity, and documentation are critical in accomplishing this objective.

Chapter 1 of the fourth edition of *Fair Housing* provides an in-depth study of the fair housing laws and how these laws relate to the real estate professional in practice. Chapter 2 explains the 1988 Fair Housing Amendments Act and focuses on discrimination involving sales, lending, and other services. Fair housing in property management is the topic in Chapter 3. Fair housing advertising is covered in Chapter 4, while Chapter 5 provides the reader with a detailed study on enforcement, standing to sue, and the use of testers. Chapter 6 covers cultural diversity and fair housing and focuses on the many aspects of working with multicultural clients. Fair housing case studies are presented in Chapter 7.

The many court cases presented throughout the book will enable the reader to understand how the courts and HUD continue to implement and interpret fair housing laws in this country.

about the author

Marcia L. Russell, DREI, president of Marcia Russell Seminars, has been a real estate educator since 1986. Marcia is a certified instructor of the Instructor Training Institute and holds the prestigious designation of Distinguished Real Estate Instructor from the Real Estate Educator's Association. She has been an REEA member since 1991.

In addition to authoring *Fair Housing*, Marcia is author of *Property Disclosures: The Real Estate Professional's Guide to Reducing Risk* and is co-author of *Risk Management*.

Marcia and her husband, Tim, own and operate T. A. Russell & Company, a property management company located in Albuquerque, New Mexico. They have four grown children and nine grandchildren.

The Fair Housing Act

We hold these truths to be self evident, that all men are created equal, that they are endowed by their Creator with certain unalienable rights, that among these are life, liberty and the pursuit of happiness. That to secure these rights, governments are instituted among men, deriving their just powers from the consent of the governed. . . .

–Declaration of Independence, adopted July 4, 1776

learning objectives

After completing this chapter, you will be able to

- list milestones in the evolution of fair housing law,
- describe discriminatory housing practices leading to the passage of the Fair Housing Act and its amendments,
- identify the classes that are provided protection under the Fair Housing Act and its amendments, and
- detail the discriminatory housing practices prohibited by the Fair Housing Act and its amendments.

Key Terms

discriminatory housing practice
dwelling
housing for older persons
protected classes
redlining
residential real estate–related transaction
steering

The Declaration of Independence, one of the greatest documents in human history, proclaimed that all people have certain human rights. The "pursuit of happiness," for most of us, means the opportunity to own our own home or to live where we choose. However, the blessings of liberty have eluded millions of Americans who have struggled through the years to attain the American Dream.

Although the signers of the Declaration stated that "all men" should be considered equal, it became apparent that persons of African descent would not be accorded any rights or freedoms. Article 1 of the United States Constitution, adopted in 1787, quantified slaves as "three-fifths" of a person in determining a state's population for Congressional representation.

The rights of African Americans were further eroded by the 1857 Supreme Court case of *Dred Scott v. Sanford*. The decision declared that no black, free or slave, could claim U.S. citizenship and that blacks had no rights that whites were bound to respect. In addition, the ruling stated that Congress could not prohibit slavery in any U.S. territory. The ruling was influential because it built angry resentment in the North and moved the nation closer to civil war. It also paved the way for the passage of the Fourteenth Amendment to the U.S. Constitution in 1868, which extended full citizenship and civil rights to African Americans. The amendment also guaranteed all persons due process and equal protection under the law.

Following the American Civil War (1861–1865), the Thirteenth Amendment, enacted in 1865, formally abolished slavery.

The following year, the Reconstruction Congress passed the Civil Rights Act of 1866, which guaranteed equal rights under the law. The act specifically provided the following:

All citizens of the United States shall have the same right, in every State and Territory, as is enjoyed by white citizens thereof to inherit, purchase, lease, sell, hold, and convey real and personal property.

For more than a century, the Civil Rights Act of 1866 would be of little importance in combating housing discrimination, primarily because courts interpreted the law to prohibit public, or governmental, discrimination only. (*See* Table 1.1.) Not until 1968 would the Supreme Court rule, in *Jones v. Mayer*, that the act "bars all racial discrimination, private as well as public, in the sale or rental of property, and that the statute, thus construed, is a valid exercise of the power of Congress to enforce the Thirteenth Amendment." Today, the act is still good law and is often used in fair housing discrimination lawsuits, especially in situations not subject to the Fair Housing Act.

In a major setback in the struggle for racial equality, the Supreme Court's 1896 decision in *Plessy v. Ferguson* opened the door for institutionalized segregation. The famous "separate but equal" doctrine legalized the separation of the races in everything from schools to public accommodations. The facilities were indeed separate, but rarely equal. The Supreme Court finally overturned the doctrine in the 1954 landmark decision in *Brown v. the Topeka Board of Education*. This ruling outlawed the separation of the races in public schools, and it was soon followed by other rulings outlawing the separation of the races. The Court made clear that all forms of government-endorsed segregation violated the Fourteenth Amendment.

In 1948, the U.S. Supreme Court held in *Shelly v. Kraemer* that enforcement of racially restrictive covenants by state courts violated the equal protection clause of the Fourteenth Amendment. Thus, persons were precluded from using the judicial system to enforce racial discrimination.

Table 1.1 | History of Residential Segregation

1920s	Whites who controlled the housing industry implemented a series of techniques designed to segregate the black population. These techniques included (1) racial zoning; (2) restrictive covenants; and (3) discriminatory sales, rental, and financing practices.
1930s	Segregation was perpetuated by federal policies that encouraged racial discrimination in federally assisted housing.
1940s–'50s–'60s	The Age of Industrialization and Urbanization brought millions of black families to cities in both the South and the North. The primary method of providing housing opportunities was through "blockbusting" neighborhoods next to ghettos.
1960s	Geographic regions throughout the United States experienced an increase in residential segregation by race.
1980s	A HUD study estimated that approximately 2 million incidents of housing discrimination were occurring every year.

It is naive to think that 50 years of segregated housing patterns and institutionalized discrimination would be reversed with the passage of this country's fair housing laws. Housing segregation has multiple causes, such as economic factors and personal preference to live with persons of the same race. However, the primary cause of the patterns of racial segregation identified in metropolitan areas must be attributed to discrimination.

The history of residential segregation in America also established the necessity to pass laws that prohibited discrimination in order to ensure a housing market that provides equal opportunity in housing to all.

On November 20, 1962, President John F. Kennedy issued Executive Order 11063, "Equal Opportunity in Housing." The order prohibited discrimination in the sale, rental, or use of all residential property that was owned, operated, or financed by the federal government. The order had little impact because it did not provide for judicial enforcement.

The Civil Rights Act of 1964 prohibited discrimination in public accommodations; in all federally assisted programs; and in employment on the basis of race, color, religion, sex, or national origin.

The year 1968 marked the beginning of the modern era of fair housing law in this country. On March 1, 1968, the National Advisory Commission on Civil Disorders published *The Kerner Report*, which showed that America was moving toward two societies, one black and one white—separate and unequal.

President Lyndon B. Johnson first introduced fair housing legislation in 1966. The three-year debate culminated in the passage of the federal Fair Housing Act. The new law was not the result of careful congressional consideration; rather, it was the product of an intense debate occurring over a relatively short period, against a background of dramatic national events. On April 4, 1968, Dr. Martin Luther King Jr. was assassinated in Memphis, Tennessee. President Johnson, in urging unity and peace, said, "America is shocked and saddened by the brutal slaying." King was the symbol of the nonviolent civil rights protest movement.

Although the Senate had passed an amended version of the Fair Housing Bill on March 11, 1968, there was little hope that the bill would pass the House of Representatives. After King's assassination, however, the House hastily passed the Fair Housing Act. President Johnson signed the Civil Rights Act of 1968 (also known as the Fair Housing Act) into law on April 11, 1968.

The 1968 law prohibited discrimination on the basis of race, color, religion, and national origin. The act was, for the most part, ineffective in combating housing discrimination. The enforcement mechanisms were simply too weak to have any perceptible impact on housing discrimination.

In 1974, Congress passed the Housing and Community Development Act, which added sex as another basis on which discrimination was prohibited. This prohibited basis includes sexual harassment but not sexual orientation. This act also created a new set of housing assistance programs for lower-income families, the Section 8 programs.

The passage of the 1988 Fair Housing Amendments Act represented the most important development in fair housing law in the 20 years since the Civil Rights Act of 1968. The number of **protected classes** expanded. (*See* Table 1.2.) Federal civil rights protections were extended to families with children and to persons with physical and mental handicaps. The 1988 Fair Housing Amendments Act radically changed the HUD enforcement procedure by adding a wide range of serious sanctions and remedies. Monetary awards were now available for actual damages as well as for noneconomic injuries such as embarrassment, humiliation, inconvenience, and mental anguish. The cap of $1,000 on punitive damages was removed in federal district court actions.

The 1995 Amendment to the Fair Housing Act repealed the significant facilities and services requirements designed to meet the physical and social needs of older persons. The 1995 amendment called on HUD to implement rules for verifying the age of occupants. The amendment also prohibits the awarding of monetary damages against persons who reasonably believed, in good faith, that the property, as **housing for older persons**, was exempt from the familial status provisions of the Fair Housing Act.

Exemptions

The Fair Housing Act contains seven exemptions with respect to property transactions not subject to the act's general mandate of nondiscriminatory treatment. It is important to note, however, that a housing provider exempt from coverage under the Fair Housing Act could still be liable for racial discrimination under the Civil

Table 1.2 | Evolution of the Protected Classes

Race, color, religion, national origin	The Fair Housing Act of 1968
Sex	The 1974 Housing and Community Development Act
Persons with physical or mental handicaps; families with children	The 1988 Fair Housing Amendments Act

Rights Act of 1866. The Civil Rights Act of 1866 is still good law and contains no exemptions to coverage.

- *Religious organizations*—A religious organization may discriminate with respect to its noncommercial property, provided that the religion itself doesn't discriminate on the basis of race, color, or national origin. The exemption also applies to a nonprofit institution operated in conjunction with a religious organization. This exemption is quite limited and has generated very little litigation.
- *Private clubs*—The act does not prohibit a private club, not in fact open to the public, from limiting the rental or occupancy of noncommercial lodgings to members. Courts have held that Congress deliberately used the word *lodging* and not **dwelling** to limit the exemption to temporary accommodations. This exemption, then, appears to be narrowly construed to cover temporary rooming facilities of social organizations, such as university clubs.
- *Occupancy standards*—The act does not limit "the applicability of any reasonable local, state, or federal restrictions regarding the maximum number of persons permitted to occupy a dwelling." The occupancy standard provision was added in 1988 at the same time families with children became a protected group and appears to be included primarily to alleviate concerns that housing providers would have to accommodate families to the extent of violating other occupancy laws.
- *Drug conviction*—The act does not prohibit conduct against a person because that person has been convicted in a court of law for the illegal manufacture or distribution of a controlled substance. This exemption was intended to allow landlords to protect tenants by refusing to provide housing to persons convicted of distributing or manufacturing illegal drugs.
- *Familial status*—Discrimination based on familial status will not apply to housing qualifying for exempt status as housing for older persons. This type of housing may allow children, but would not violate fair housing laws by excluding them. Racial and other prohibited forms of discrimination are not allowed in the housing for older persons. The exemptions for housing for older persons include the following:
  - Housing provided under any state or federal program that the secretary of HUD has determined is specifically designed and operated to assist elderly persons
  - Housing intended for and solely occupied by persons 62 years of age or older
  - Housing intended and operated for occupancy by at least one person 55 years of age or older per unit in at least 80 percent of the units
- *Single-family housing*—The sale or rental of a single-family house by the owner will be exempt from coverage, provided that the following conditions are met:
  - The owner does not own or have any interest in more than three single-family houses at any one time.
  - The house is sold or rented without the services of a real estate agent or the facilities of any person in the business of selling or renting dwellings. The exemption will apply to one sale or rental within a two-year period, unless the owner was the most recent occupant.

  This exemption does not apply if a person in the real estate business is involved or if discriminatory advertising is used.

- *Mrs. Murphy's exemption*—The act does not cover owner-occupied dwellings designed for occupancy by no more than four families living independently of each other.

  It must be remembered that a single-family homeowner, or a "Mrs. Murphy," is still liable for racial discrimination under the Civil Rights Act of 1866.

Discriminatory Housing Practices

The Fair Housing Act prohibits the following **discriminatory housing practices**[1]:

- To refuse to sell or rent after the making of a bona fide offer, or to refuse to negotiate for the sale or rental of, or otherwise make unavailable or deny, a dwelling to any person because of race, color, religion, sex, familial status, or national origin
- To discriminate against any person in the terms, conditions, or privileges of sale or rental of a dwelling, or in the provision of services or facilities in connection therewith, because of race, color, religion, sex, familial status, or national origin

---

Note:

The first two provisions do not include handicap as a protected class. The 1988 Fair Housing Amendments Act added several new provisions that deal exclusively with protections for this class. The reason for treating handicap discrimination in this way was apparently to clarify that the law does not condemn housing that is available only to persons with physical or mental disabilities.

- To make, print, or publish, or cause to be made, printed, or published any notice, statement, or advertisement, with respect to the sale or rental of a dwelling, that indicates any preference, limitation, or discrimination based on race, color, religion, sex, handicap, familial status, or national origin, or an intention to make any such preference, limitation, or discrimination
- To represent to any person because of race, color, religion, sex, handicap, familial status, or national origin that any dwelling is not available for inspection, sale, or rental when such dwelling is in fact so available
- For profit, to induce or attempt to induce any person to sell or rent any dwelling by representation regarding the entry or prospective entry into the neighborhood of a person or persons of a particular race, color, religion, sex, handicap, familial status, or national origin
- To discriminate in the sale or rental, or to otherwise make unavailable or deny, a dwelling to any buyer or renter because of a handicap of
  - that buyer or renter;
  - a person residing in or intending to reside in that dwelling after it is so sold, rented, or made available; or
  - any person associated with that buyer or renter

---

1 The listed discriminatory housing practices are quoted from 42 U.S.C. §§ 3601–3619.

- To discriminate against any person in the terms, conditions, or privileges of sale or rental of a dwelling, or in the provision of services or facilities in connection with such dwelling, because of a handicap of
  - that buyer or renter;
  - a person residing in or intending to reside in that dwelling after it is so sold, rented, or made available; or
  - any person associated with that buyer or renter
- To refuse to permit, at the expense of the handicapped person, reasonable modifications of existing premises occupied or to be occupied by such person if such modifications may be necessary to afford such person full enjoyment of the premises, except that in the case of a rental, the landlord may, where it is reasonable to do so, condition permission for a modification on the renter agreeing to restore the interior of the premises to the condition that existed before the modification, reasonable wear and tear excepted
- To refuse to make reasonable accommodations in rules, policies, practices, or services, when such accommodations may be necessary to afford a handicapped person equal opportunity to use or enjoy the dwelling
- To fail to design and construct covered multifamily dwellings for first occupancy after March 12, 1991, that are accessible to and usable by handicapped persons
- To deny any person access to or membership or participation in any multiple-listing service, real estate brokers' organization, or other service, organization, or facility relating to the business of selling or renting dwellings, or to discriminate in the terms or conditions of such access, membership, or participation, on account of race, color, religion, sex, handicap, familial status, or national origin
- For persons whose business includes engaging in residential real estate–related transactions, to discriminate against any person in making available such a transaction, or in the terms or conditions of such a transaction, because of race, color, religion, sex, handicap, familial status, or national origin

HUD Regulations

The 1988 Fair Housing Amendments Act contains provisions giving HUD the authority to issue rules to implement the Fair Housing Act. HUD's regulations are based, in part, on 20 years of housing discrimination cases originating under the 1968 act. In 1972, the Supreme Court ruled in *Trafficante v. Metropolitan Life Insurance Co.*, the very first decision involving the Civil Rights Act of 1968, that interpretations of the act by HUD are entitled to a good deal of weight in construing the statute. This is because HUD is the primary agency responsible for implementing and administering the act. The regulations went into effect on March 12, 1989, and provide a tremendous amount of authoritative material concerning the meaning of the Fair Housing Act.[2]

---

2 Provisions of the Fair Housing Amendments Act noted in this section are adapted or quoted from 42 U.S.C. §§ 3601 *et seq.*

Unlawful to Sell or Rent or to Negotiate for the Sale or Rental

Prohibited actions under this section include the following:

- Failing to accept or consider a bona fide offer because of race, color, religion, sex, handicap, familial status, or national origin
- Refusing to sell or rent a dwelling to, or negotiate for the sale or rental of a dwelling with, any person because of protected class status
- Imposing different sales prices or rental charges for the sale or rental of a dwelling upon any person because of membership in a protected class
- Using different qualification criteria or applications, or sale or rental standards or procedures, such as income standards, application requirements, application fees, credit analysis, or sale or rental approval procedures, based on protected class status
- Evicting tenants because of their race, color, religion, sex, handicap, familial status, or national origin, or because their guests are members of a protected class

Discrimination in Terms, Conditions, and Privileges, and in Services and Facilities

Prohibited actions under this section include the following:

- Using different provisions in leases or contracts of sale, such as those relating to rental charges, security deposits, and the terms of a lease, and those relating to down payment and closing requirements, because of race, color, religion, sex, handicap, familial status, or national origin
- Failing or delaying maintenance or repairs of sale or rental dwellings because of membership in a protected group
- Failing to process an offer for the sale or rental of a dwelling or to communicate an offer accurately because of protected class status
- Limiting the use of privileges, services, or facilities associated with a dwelling because of race, color, religion, sex, handicap, familial status, or national origin
- Denying or limiting services or facilities in connection with sale or rental of a dwelling because a person failed or refused to provide sexual favors

Other Prohibited Sale and Rental Conduct

Prohibited actions under this section include the following:

- Restricting or attempting to restrict the choices of a person by word or conduct in connection with seeking, negotiating for, buying, or renting a dwelling so as to perpetuate, or tend to perpetuate, segregated housing patterns based on membership in a protected class
- Engaging in any conduct related to the provision of housing or of services or facilities that otherwise makes unavailable or denies dwellings to protected persons
- Discouraging any person from inspecting, purchasing, or renting a dwelling on account of race, color, religion, sex, handicap, familial status, or national origin by exaggerating drawbacks and failing to inform any person of desirable features of a dwelling or neighborhood
- Communicating to any persons that they would not be compatible with existing residents of a community because of their protected class status

- Assigning any person to a particular section of a community, neighborhood, or dwelling, or to a particular floor of a building because of race, color, religion, sex, handicap, familial status, or national origin, a practice also known as **steering**
- Employing codes or other devices to segregate or reject applicants, purchasers, or renters or refusing to take or show listings of dwellings in certain areas because of race, color, religion, sex, handicap, familial status, or national origin
- Refusing to provide municipal services or property or hazard insurance for dwellings or providing such services or insurance differently because of race, color, religion, sex, handicap, familial status, or national origin

The HUD Regulations dealing with discriminatory advertisements, statements, and notices are presented in detail in Chapter 4.

Discriminatory Representations on the Availability of Dwellings

Prohibited actions under this section include the following:

- Indicating through words or conduct that a dwelling that is available for inspection, sale, or rental has been sold or rented
- Representing that covenants, or other deed, trust, or lease provisions that purport to restrict the sale or rental of dwellings because of protected class status, preclude the sale or rental of a dwelling to any person from a protected class
- Enforcing covenants or other deed, trust, or lease provisions that preclude the sale or rental of a dwelling to any person because of membership in a protected class
- Limiting information, by word or conduct, regarding suitably priced dwellings available for inspection, sale, or rental to members of a protected group
- Providing false or inaccurate information regarding the availability of a dwelling for sale or rental to any person, including testers, regardless of whether such person is actually seeking housing, based on protected class status

Blockbusting

Prohibited actions under this section include the following:

- For profit, to induce or attempt to induce a person to sell or rent a dwelling by representations regarding the entry or prospective entry into the neighborhood of members of a particular protected group
- In establishing a discriminatory housing practice under this section, it is not necessary that there was in fact profit, as long as profit was a factor for engaging in the blockbusting activity
- Engaging in conduct, including uninvited solicitations, that conveys to a person that a neighborhood is undergoing or is about to undergo a change in the race, color religion, sex, handicap, familial status, or national origin to encourage the person to offer a dwelling for sale or rental
- Encouraging any person to sell or rent a dwelling by asserting that the entry or prospective entry of persons of a particular protected class will result in undesirable consequences for the project, neighborhood, or community, such as an increase in criminal or antisocial behavior or a decline in the quality of schools or other services or facilities

Discrimination in Residential Real Estate–Related Transactions

It is illegal for any person or other entity whose business includes engaging in residential real estate–related transactions to discriminate against any person in making available such a transaction or to make changes in the terms or conditions of the transaction because of a person's status in a protected class. The term **residential real estate–related transaction** means

- the making or purchasing of loans or providing other financial assistance for purchasing, constructing, improving, or maintaining a dwelling (included in this section are loans secured by residential real estate); and
- the selling, brokering, or appraising of residential real property.

Prohibited actions under this section include the following:

- Refusing to provide information to any person concerning the availability of loans or other financial assistance or providing information that is inaccurate or different because of membership in a protected class
- Refusing to purchase loans, debts, or securities or imposing different terms and conditions for such purchase to persons of a protected group
- Using different policies, practices, or procedures in evaluating or determining creditworthiness of any person in connection with the provision of any loan or other financial assistance for a dwelling because that person is a member of a protected class
- Determining the type of loan or other financial assistance to be provided with respect to a dwelling or fixing the amount, interest rate, duration, or other terms for the loan or other financial assistance because of membership in a protected group

---

Note:

The term **redlining** refers to the practice of refusing to make loans or otherwise denying financial assistance for housing in particular areas. The courts have defined *redlining* as mortgage credit discrimination based on the characteristics of the neighborhood surrounding the would-be borrower's dwelling. The term was derived from the practice of loan officers who would evaluate home mortgage applications by relying on a residential map where integrated and minority areas were marked off in red as poor risk areas.

The Fair Housing Act also prohibits insurance redlining, discriminating in the provision of homeowners' insurance based on the characteristics of the neighborhood where the home is situated.

Unlawful practices in the selling, brokering, or appraising of residential real property include

- an appraisal that improperly takes into consideration race, color, religion, sex, handicap, familial status, or national origin in estimating value; and
- using an appraisal that improperly takes into consideration the protected classes in estimating value in connection with the sale, rental, or financing of a dwelling where the person knows or reasonably should know that the appraisal was based on discriminatory factors.

Nothing in this section prohibits a person engaged in the business of making or furnishing appraisals of residential real property from taking into consideration factors other than race, color, religion, sex, handicap, familial status, or national origin.

Note:

Section 818 of the Fair Housing Act makes it unlawful to "coerce, intimidate, threaten, or interfere with any person in the exercise or enjoyment of, or on account of his having exercised or enjoyed, or on account of his having aided or encouraged any other person in the exercise or enjoyment of any right granted or protected by" the statute.

HUD Issues Guidance on Lesbian, Gay, Bisexual and Transgender (LGBT) Housing Discrimination Complaints

"On July 1, 2010, HUD announced a new policy that provides LGBT individuals and families with further assistance when facing housing discrimination. The new guidance treats gender identity discrimination as gender discrimination under the Fair Housing Act, and instructs HUD staff to inform individuals filing complaints about state and local agencies that have LGBT-inclusive discrimination laws," according to HUD press release no. 10-139. Approximately 20 states and the District of Columbia and, as well as more than 200 cities, towns, and counties have additional protections that prohibit discrimination against LGBT individuals.
The HUD press release provides examples of situations that may be jurisdictional under the Fair Housing Act. These examples are as follows:

- "If a man alleges that he is being evicted because he is gay and his landlord believes he will infect other tenants with HIV, then the allegation of discrimination may be jurisdictional under the Fair Housing Act based on disability, because the man is regarded as having a disability, HIV/AIDS."
- "Similarly, if a female prospective tenant is alleging discrimination by a landlord because she wears masculine clothes and engages in other physical expressions that are stereotypically male, then the allegations may be jurisdictional under the Act as discrimination based on gender."

Equal Access to Housing in HUD Programs Regardless of Sexual Orientation or Gender Identity

According to HUD, "this final rule, effective March 5, 2012, HUD implements policy to ensure that its core programs are open to all eligible individuals and families regardless of sexual orientation, gender identity, or marital status." Owners and operators of HUD-funded housing, or housing insured by HUD are prohibited from inquiring about an applicant's sexual orientation or gender identity, or denying housing on that basis.

The term *family* is slightly reorganized in the opening clause to read as follows: "Family includes but is not limited to the following, regardless of actual or perceived sexual orientation, gender identity, or marital status."

The rule adds sexual orientation and gender identity to the characteristics that an FHA lender may not take into consideration in determining the adequacy of a mortgagor's income.

The language of the final rule says that "it is important not only that HUD ensure that its own programs do not involve discrimination against any individual or family otherwise eligible for HUD-assisted or -insured housing, but that its policies and programs serve as models for equal housing opportunity." The final rule as published in the Federal Register can be accessed at *www.gpo.gov/fdsys/pkg/FR-2012-02-03/html/2012-2343.htm*.

The HUD Web site can be accessed at *www.hud.gov/fairhousing*. This site provides additional contact information, and the brochure *Fair Housing—Equal Opportunity for All* may be downloaded at *www.hud.gov/offices/adm/hudclips/forms/files/1686.pdf*.

State and Local Fair Housing Laws

Most states and many localities have some form of fair housing law, and it is important to be aware that they exist as an independent source of housing discrimination law. As a rule, the remedies provided by state or local fair housing law to private victims of discrimination are independent of their rights under federal law. This means that the victim of an act of housing discrimination is allowed to file separate federal and state law claims for the same unlawful discriminatory act without having to choose between the federal and state remedies.

Using the state procedure may be more convenient and less expensive than filing a federal lawsuit. The complainant does not have to hire an attorney. In addition there may be substantive advantages in using the state or local system. While the federal law bans discrimination based on race, color, religion, sex, national origin, handicap, and familial status, many state and local laws go beyond this to prohibit discrimination directed at a variety of other groups. Licensees should be aware of all of the protected classes, both locally and at the state level. Additional protected groups may include age, marital status sexual orientation, gender identity, source of income, military record, and so forth.

When federal law conflicts with state or local fair housing law, the law that imposes the most constraints or places the greater burden prevails. For example, under federal law, transvestites are exempted from the definition of disability and, therefore, are not considered a protected group. In New Mexico, however, gender identity is a protected class and is defined in the statute to mean "a person's self-perception, or perception . . . by another, of the person's identity as male or female based on the person's appearance, behavior, or physical characteristics that are in accord with or opposed to the person's physical anatomy, chromosomal sex, or sex at birth."

Claims based on state or local fair housing laws are subject to the jurisdictional requirements and other procedures set out in those laws, which generally means that they may be brought only in state court or in a state or local agency.

It is important to note that a state statute may stand ready to revoke the real estate license of a defendant found guilty of housing discrimination.

States may impose more severe penalties for violations. For instance, Virginia's penalty for a first offense is $50,000 and up to $100,000 for a second offense.

Summary

Table 1.3 summarizes the history of fair housing legislation in the United States. In order to avoid a fair housing complaint, today's real estate professional must have an in-depth understanding of the Fair Housing Act and the HUD regulations that further define the law. Agents must be willing to educate both buyers and sellers in the provisions of the law, as well as in the penalties for noncompliance. If, at any time, a seller appears to be considering discriminating against a potential buyer for any reason, the agent should point out that the action would violate the Fair Housing Act. If sellers are unwilling to offer their home to all protected groups on an equal basis, the real estate professional has no choice but to decline or cancel the listing.

Buyer's agents also need to be aware that if their client expresses intent to limit the housing search based on protected class factors, they too may find themselves involved in litigation.

case study

Salesperson Matt Henry listed a property for sale by owners Bob and Patty Brown. Henry told the Browns that their home would be listed in the multiple listing service and informed them of the Fair Housing Act and its prohibitions against discrimination based on race, color, religion, sex, familial status, and national origin. The Browns signed all the paperwork and Henry proceeded to market their property, advertising in the local newspaper and holding open houses to generate interest.

At one of the open houses, an African American couple, Anthony and Debra Johnson, expressed interest in the property and decided to make an offer through Henry. The sellers asked Henry to disclose the race of the buyers. Henry did so, and at this point, the sellers refused to negotiate with the Johnsons because of their race.

Henry terminated the listing agreement and informed the Johnsons of their right to file a fair housing complaint against the sellers. He assisted them in filing a complaint with HUD.

1. Which discriminatory practice occurred here?
2. Did Henry violate the Fair Housing Act when he disclosed the race of the buyers?

Table 1.3 | Historical Overview of Fair Housing Legislation in America

Year	Legislation	Description
1787	U.S. Constitution	Quantified slaves as three-fifths of a person
1791	Bill of Rights	First ten amendments to the Constitution, including freedom of speech and the press, the right to due process, and the right of free exercise of religion
1857	Dred Scott Decision	Blacks denied U.S. citizenship
1865	Thirteenth Amendment	Abolished slavery
1866	Civil Rights Act of 1866	Guaranteed all citizens equal rights under the law
1868	Fourteenth Amendment	Extended full citizenship to persons of African descent; guaranteed all persons due process and equal protection
1896	*Plessy v. Ferguson*	Supreme Court decision establishing "separate but equal" doctrine
1948	*Shelly v. Kraemer*	Supreme Court decision barring state courts from enforcing racially restrictive covenants
1954	*Brown v. Board of Education*	Supreme Court decision overturning the "separate but equal" doctrine as applied to public schools
1962	Executive Order 11063	Antidiscrimination mandate directed to all federal agencies
1964	Civil Rights Act of 1964	Prohibited discrimination in public accommodations; in federally assisted programs; and in employment on the basis of race, color, religion, sex, or national origin
1968	Kerner Report	Reported America was moving toward two societies, one black and one white—separate and unequal
1968	The Civil Rights Act of 1968	Prohibited discrimination on the basis of race, color, religion, and national origin
1968	*Jones v. Mayer*	Supreme Court decision ruling that the Civil Rights Act of 1866 applies to private as well as public discrimination
1973	Rehabilitation Act of 1973	Prohibited discrimination against persons with disabilities in all federally assisted programs, including housing
1974	Housing and Community Development Act	Added sex as another basis on which discrimination is prohibited
1988	The 1988 Fair Housing Amendments Act	Added familial status and physical and mental handicap as protected classes; greatly strengthened enforcement mechanisms
1995	Amendment to Fair Housing Act	Repealed the significant services and facilities requirement for housing to qualify for exemption as "housing for older persons"
2010	Gender nonconformity or sex stereotyping is considered sex discrimination	HUD staff must inform individuals filing complaints about State and local protections
2012	Equal access in housing in HUD programs, regardless of sexual orientation or gender identity	New rule protecting LGBT persons from discrimination in HUD programs; in addition, housing providers who receive HUD funding, have loans insured by the Federal Housing Administration (FHA), as well as lenders insured by FHA are subject to HUD program regulations

Chapter 1 Review Questions

1. The Civil Rights Act of 1866 prohibits discrimination on the basis of
   a. national origin.
   b. race.
   c. sex.
   d. religion.

2. The famous "separate but equal" doctrine is from which of the following Supreme Court decisions?
   a. *Jones v. Mayer*
   b. *Shelley v. Kraemer*
   c. *Plessy v. Ferguson*
   d. *Brown v. the Board of Education*

3. The Supreme Court decision that interpreted the Civil Rights Act of 1866 to prohibit discrimination in both the public and private sectors was
   a. *Shelly v. Kraemer.*
   b. *Plessy v. Ferguson.*
   c. the *Dred Scott* decision.
   d. *Jones v. Mayer.*

4. Sex was added as a protected class by the
   a. 1988 Fair Housing Amendments Act.
   b. 1968 Fair Housing Act.
   c. 1974 Housing and Community Development Act.
   d. Civil Rights Act of 1964.

5. The 1968 Fair Housing Act was signed into law by President
   a. John F. Kennedy.
   b. Lyndon B. Johnson.
   c. Richard M. Nixon.
   d. Ronald Reagan.

6. All of the following would be exempt from coverage from the Fair Housing Act *EXCEPT*
   a. noncommercial property owned by a religious organization.
   b. lodging provided to members of a private club.
   c. a non-owner-occupied fourplex.
   d. single-family housing meeting certain restrictions.

7. Discriminatory housing practices include all of the following *EXCEPT*
   a. blockbusting.
   b. steering.
   c. showing only currently available property.
   d. refusing to rent to a family with children.

8. The illegal practice of steering includes all of the following *EXCEPT*
   a. indicating that a person would not be compatible living in a certain area.
   b. exaggerating the drawbacks of an area.
   c. showing only properties selected by the prospect.
   d. attempting to restrict the choices of a homeseeker.

9. Which of the following statements is *TRUE* regarding the Fair Housing Act?
   a. There must be profit for blockbusting to occur.
   b. An appraisal may consider protected class status when estimating value.
   c. The act permits housing providers to assign families to ground-floor units for safety reasons.
   d. According to HUD, failing to inform a person of desirable features of a dwelling possibly violates the act.

10. The Fair Housing Act prohibits all of the following *EXCEPT*
    a. refusing to rent an apartment to a convicted drug dealer.
    b. excluding families with children.
    c. using different sales contracts and leases based on race or other protected class factors.
    d. using an appraisal that considers factors associated with the protected classes.

chapter two

The 1988 Amendments Act and Beyond

learning objectives

After completing this chapter, you will be able to

- examine the changes made in enforcement,
- understand familial status discrimination,
- explain how the Fair Housing Act is applied to both the banking and insurance industries, and
- discuss the HUD regulations concerning handicap and familial status.

Key Terms

familial status
handicap
major life activities
multifamily dwelling

The 1988 Fair Housing Amendments Act, the most important development in housing discrimination law since the passage of the Fair Housing Act in 1968, extended federal civil rights protection to families with children and to persons with physical and mental disabilities. The act also greatly strengthened the enforcement mechanisms and gave the Department of Housing and Urban Development (HUD) greater enforcement power. The underlying assumption was that the enforcement and remedies available under the 1968 act were simply too weak to combat housing discrimination. This was evidenced by a HUD study done in the late 1970s that led HUD to conclude that approximately 2 million incidents of housing discrimination were occurring each year.

The 1988 Fair Housing Amendments Act passed by overwhelming margins in both the House and the Senate, and was signed into law by President Ronald Reagan on September 13, 1988. The effective date of the act was March 12, 1989.

With the passage of the 1988 Amendments Act, the fair housing laws were applied to the banking and insurance industries for the first time. This chapter will focus on discriminatory practices in sales, lending, and provision of services.

Summary of Changes Made in Enforcement

The 1988 Fair Housing Amendments Act provided major changes in federal district court actions. The statute of limitations was extended from 180 days to two years, and restrictions on punitive damages and attorney's fees were removed. Prior to the passage of the new law, there had been a cap of $1,000 on punitive damages. The removal of the cap cleared the way for unlimited damage awards. The 1988 act also made attorney's fees available to prevailing plaintiffs. The 1968 act authorized fees awards to only those prevailing plaintiffs who were financially unable to pay.

The 1988 act transformed the HUD enforcement procedure from an ineffective system of conciliation and persuasion to a body providing administrative and judicial hearings complete with a full range of serious sanctions and remedies. The statute of limitations was extended from 180 days to one year, and civil penalties of up to $50,000 may now be assessed in a HUD proceeding.

Relief available in lawsuits by the Justice Department was expanded by the 1988 act to include monetary awards and civil penalties of up to $100,000. The law also provided for a good deal more coordination between the three enforcement systems. For example, a complainant who elected to have the case decided in a HUD administrative hearing would be precluded from pursuing the matter further in federal district court.

Application of the Fair Housing Laws to the Banking Industry

Discrimination in mortgage lending is prohibited by the federal Fair Housing Act, and HUD's Office of Fair Housing and Equal Opportunity actively enforces those provisions of the law. The Fair Housing Act makes it unlawful to engage in the following practices based on race, color, national origin, religion, sex, familial status, or handicap (disability). In 2012, HUD implemented a new rule that prohibits FHA lenders from considering a person's sexual orientation or gender identity in determining the adequacy of a mortgagor's income.

- Refusal to make a mortgage loan
- Refusal to provide information regarding loans
- Imposition of different terms or conditions on a loan, such as different interest rates, points, or fees
- Discrimination in appraising property
- Refusal to purchase a loan or set different terms or conditions for purchasing a loan

Justice Department Reaches Agreement with Countrywide Financial

On December 21, 2011, the Department of Justice

filed its largest residential fair lending settlement in history to resolve allegations that Countrywide Financial Corporation and its subsidiaries engaged in a widespread pattern or practice of discrimination against qualified African-American and Hispanic borrowers in their mortgage lending from 2004 through 2008.

The settlement provides $335 million in compensation for victims of Countrywide's discrimination during a period when Countrywide originated millions of residential mortgage loans as one of the nation's largest single-family mortgage lenders.

The settlement, which is subject to court approval, was filed in the U.S. District Court for the Central District of California in conjunction with the department's complaint. . . . "With [the] settlement, the federal government will ensure that the more than 200,000 African-American and Hispanic borrowers who were discriminated against by Countrywide will be entitled to compensation, [said Attorney General Eric Holder]. The settlement resolves the United States' pricing and steering claims against Countrywide for its discrimination against African Americans and Hispanics.

The United States' complaint alleges that African-American and Hispanic borrowers paid more than non-Hispanic white borrowers, not based on borrower risk, but because of their race or national origin. Countrywide's business practice allowed its loan officers and mortgage brokers to vary a loan's interest rate and other fees from the price it set based on the borrower's objective credit-related factors. This subjective and unguided pricing discretion resulted in African American and Hispanic borrowers paying more. The complaint further alleges that Countrywide was aware the fees and interest rates it was charging discriminated against African-American and Hispanic borrowers, but failed to impose meaningful limits or guidelines to stop it. . . .

The United States' complaint also alleges that, as a result of Countrywide's policies and practices, qualified African-American and Hispanic borrowers were placed in subprime loans rather than prime loans even when similarly-qualified non-Hispanic white borrowers were placed in prime loans. The discriminatory placement of borrowers in subprime loans, also known as "steering," occurred because it was Countrywide's business practice to allow mortgage brokers and employees to place a loan applicant in a subprime loan even when the applicant qualified for a prime loan. In addition, Countrywide gave mortgage brokers discretion to request exceptions to the underwriting guidelines, and Countrywide's employees had discretion to grant these exceptions. . . .

The settlement also resolves the department's claim that Countrywide violated the Equal Credit Opportunity Act by discriminating on the basis of marital status against non-applicant spouses of borrowers by encouraging them to sign away their home ownership rights. The law allows married individuals to apply for credit either in their own name or jointly with their spouse, even when the property is owned by both spouses. For applications made by married individuals applying solely in their own name between 2004 and 2008, Countrywide encouraged non-applicant spouses to sign quitclaim deeds or other documents transferring their legal rights and interests in jointly-held property to the borrowing spouse. Non-applicant spouses who execute a quitclaim deed risk substantial uncertainty and financial loss by losing all their rights and interests in the property securing the loan.[1]

Predatory Lending

Some lenders, often called predatory lenders, saddle borrowers with loans that come with outrageous terms and conditions, often through deception. Elderly women and minorities frequently report that they have been targeted, or preyed on, by these lenders. The typical predatory loan is (1) in excess of those available to similarly situated borrowers from other lenders elsewhere in the lending market, (2) not justified by the creditworthiness of the borrower or the risk of loss, and (3) secured by the borrower's home. HUD is working hard to fight predatory lending.

Minority Homeownership

HUD is committed to increasing homeownership opportunities for all Americans. HUD is engaged in a special effort to boost the minority homeownership rate because the rate for black and Hispanic Americans lags behind that of others. Read more about HUD's efforts to increase minority homeownership at the HUD Web site: *www.hud.gov.*

The Equal Credit Opportunity Act

The Equal Credit Opportunity Act (ECOA) makes it unlawful for any creditor to discriminate against any applicant, with respect to any aspect of a credit transaction,

- on the basis of race, color, religion, national origin, sex, marital status, or age, provided that the applicant has the capacity to contract;
- because all or part of the applicant's income derives from any public assistance program; or
- because the applicant has in good faith exercised any right under the Consumer Credit Protection Act.

1 U.S. Department of Justice, Office of Public Affairs, "Justice Department Reaches $335 Million Settlement to Resolve Allegations of Lending Discrimination by Countrywide Financial Corporation," 21 December 2011, *www.justice.gov/opa/pr/2011/December/11-ag-1694.html.*

The ECOA requires that a creditor notify an applicant of its action on a completed credit application within 30 days after receipt of the application and, if that action is adverse, provide the applicant with a statement of the specific reasons for such action.

The ECOA applies to housing in at least two important ways. First, it covers applications for mortgages and other forms of credit in the housing field. Second, it has been held to provide a right of action for residents living in segregated neighborhoods who have been denied credit because of the racial makeup of their area. Provisions of the Fair Housing Act prohibit these types of credit discrimination, but the ECOA does extend protection to other groups based on marital status and age.

The act authorizes various methods of enforcement, including "pattern or practice" suits by the attorney general and private actions by aggrieved persons for actual damages, punitive damages of not more than $10,000, equitable and declaratory relief, and reasonable attorney's fees and costs. The act provides for a two-year statute of limitations and for federal court jurisdiction without regard to the amount in controversy.

New Mexico Bank Settles National Origin Claims with $585,000 Agreement with Justice Department

The Justice Department alleged that the First National Bank (FNB) had violated fair lending laws by giving less favorable treatment to Hispanic mortgage applicants than it gave to white applicants. According to the complaint, the bank had been approving white applicants for home loans while rejecting similarly qualified Hispanic applicants from January 1992 through March 1995. The complaint further alleged that white applicants were given opportunities to explain past credit problems and outside sources of other income, while Hispanic applicants with credit problems were simply rejected. In some cases, FNB did not even attempt to verify the credit references on loan applications from Hispanic customers.

Hispanic applicants were also being denied because they had not lived in the bank's service area long enough or had no history of established credit. Whites with poor credit were being approved and the bank's argument to the Justice Department was that a poor credit history was better than no history at all.

FNB agreed to establish a $485,000 fund to compensate Hispanic applicants to whom it wrongfully denied loans. The bank also agreed to create a $750,000 fund to allow applicants purchasing mobile homes to do so at reduced interest rates. The bank's estimated cost to establish the fund was set at $100,000, a figure agreed to in the settlement.

Application of Fair Housing Laws to the Insurance Industry

One of the practices identified in the HUD regulations as violating the Fair Housing Act is that of "refusing to provide . . . property or hazard insurance for dwellings or providing such . . . insurance differently because of race, color, religion, sex, handicap, familial status, or national origin." This regulation may also be interpreted to include insurance practices that are based on the race (or another prohibited characteristic) makeup of the neighborhood where the dwelling is located.

The dispute over whether the Fair Housing Act applies to insurance and insurance redlining is an important one. In 1997, Allstate and Nationwide insurance companies resolved complaints of discrimination in the underwriting of homeowners' insurance. Both companies agreed to eliminate underwriting guidelines based on minimum dollar amounts and to expand their businesses in minority urban areas. Nationwide did not admit liability and maintains that the Fair Housing Act does not apply to property insurance carriers.

American Family Settles Insurance Bias Lawsuit for Record $16 Million—U.S. v. American Family Insurance Co. No. 95-C0327

In 1990, the Justice Department, the NAACP, and seven African American Milwaukee homeowners sued American Family Mutual Insurance Company for redlining predominantly black areas of Milwaukee and offering inferior coverage to black homeowners compared with whites. The 7th Circuit ruled in 1992 that the Fair Housing Act applies to homeowners' insurance, a ruling that was crucial for the plaintiffs in this case. The complaint stated that American Family offered insurance to blacks at higher rates and on less advantageous terms. American Family had no desire for business in predominantly black areas of Milwaukee and trained underwriters to consider homes within the African American community as a negative factor. The sales force at American Family was overwhelmingly white. The settlement includes $5 million for aggrieved persons, $9.5 million for housing programs to benefit low and moderate-income persons in predominantly black areas of Milwaukee, $10,000 each to the NAACP and the seven plaintiffs, and a total of $2 million in attorney's fees and litigation costs. American Family must also revise underwriting guidelines, adhere to extensive record keeping and reporting requirements, conduct testing, and advertise in black-oriented publications.

Familial Status Discrimination

The Fair Housing Act makes no distinction between the level of protection afforded to victims of familial status discrimination and that afforded victims of racial discrimination. HUD regulations state that "families with children must be provided the same protections as other classes of persons" protected by the Fair Housing Act. Housing providers remain free, however, to refuse to deal with families based on legitimate criteria, such as evicting a family because of excessive noise or property damage that can be attributed to their children.

The law broadly defines **familial status** to include anyone younger than 18 being domiciled with

- a parent or another person having legal custody of such individual or
- the designee of such parent or other person having such custody with the written permission of such parent or other person.

The protections against discrimination on the basis of familial status also apply to any person who is pregnant or in the process of securing legal custody of any individual younger than 18.

The Fair Housing Act's ban on family status discrimination also prohibits advertising that indicates any preference, limitation, or discrimination based on protected class status. Thus, photographs or words indicating that children are not welcome would be actionable under the law. Conversely, phrases such as "kids ok" would show an illegal preference for families with children.

Housing for Older Persons Act of 1995

The Housing for Older Persons Act of 1995 (HOPA) makes several changes to the 55-and-older exemption. Since the 1988 Amendments, the Fair Housing Act has exempted from its familial status provisions properties that satisfy the act's 55-and-older housing condition.

First, it eliminates the requirement that 55-and-older housing have "significant facilities and services" designed for the elderly. Second, HOPA establishes a "good-faith reliance" immunity from damages for persons who in good faith believe that the 55-and-older exemption applies to a particular property, if they do not actually know that the property is not eligible for the exemption and if the property has formally stated in writing that it qualifies for the exemption.

HOPA retains the requirement that senior housing must have one person who is 55 years of age or older living in at least 80 percent of its occupied units. It also still requires that senior housing publish and follow policies and procedures that demonstrate an intent to be housing for persons 55 and older. An exempt property will not violate the Fair Housing Act if it includes families with children, but it does not have to do so.

A HUD rule published in the April 2, 1999, Federal Register implements HOPA and explains in detail those provisions of the Fair Housing Act that pertain to senior housing.

Disability Discrimination

The Congress that passed the 1988 Fair Housing Amendments Act recognized the need to define and protect the rights of the disabled throughout American society. Persons with physical and mental disabilities had been denied housing because of misperceptions, ignorance, and outright prejudice. The decision to add disability discrimination to the Fair Housing Amendments Act was seen as a strong statement concerning the exclusion of persons with disabilities from the American mainstream. A House Judiciary Committee Report stated that the new law "repudiates the use of stereotypes and ignorance, and mandates that persons with handicaps be considered as individuals."

The 1988 Fair Housing Amendments Act defined the term *handicap* very broadly, and added prohibitions against discrimination based on handicap to nearly every existing provision of the act. In addition, several new provisions were added that deal exclusively with disability discrimination. Much of the language and definitions contained in the 1988 Fair Housing Amendments Act can be traced to the Rehabilitation Act of 1973. The act prohibits discrimination against the disabled in programs or activities that receive federal financial assistance, including housing programs receiving federal funds.

Definition of Handicap

The Fair Housing Act defines **handicap** as

- a physical or mental impairment that substantially limits one or more of a person's major life activities,
- a record of having such an impairment, or
- being regarded as having such an impairment.

Nothing in the Fair Housing Act requires that a dwelling be made available to an individual whose tenancy would constitute a direct threat to the health or safety of other individuals, or whose tenancy would result in substantial physical damage to the property of others.

The definition excludes transvestites and persons who are engaging in the illegal use of drugs.

A physical impairment is any physiological disorder or condition, cosmetic disfigurement, or anatomical loss affecting one or more of the following body systems: neurological; musculoskeletal; specific sense organs; respiratory (including speech organs); cardiovascular; reproductive; digestive; genitourinary; hematologic and lymphatic; skin; and endocrine.

A mental impairment is any mental or psychological disorder, such as mental retardation, organic brain syndrome, emotional or mental illness, and specific learning disabilities.

HUD regulations define the term *physical or mental impairment* to include, but not be limited to, such diseases and conditions as orthopedic, visual, speech, and hearing impairments; cerebral palsy; autism; epilepsy; muscular dystrophy; multiple sclerosis; cancer; heart disease; diabetes; human immunodeficiency virus infection; mental retardation; emotional illness; drug addiction (other than addiction caused by current illegal use of a controlled substance); and alcoholism.

Major life activities means functions such as caring for oneself, performing manual tasks, walking, seeing, hearing, speaking, breathing, learning, and working.

HUD Regulations

HUD regulations and the Fair Housing Act contain the same general prohibitions against discrimination because of handicap. Prohibited actions under this section are as follows:

- To discriminate in the sale or rental of, or to otherwise make unavailable or deny, a dwelling to any buyer or renter because of a handicap of
  - that buyer or renter;
  - a person residing in or intending to reside in that dwelling after it is so sold, rented, or made available; or
  - any person associated with that buyer or renter.
- To discriminate against any person in the terms, conditions, or privileges of sale or rental of a dwelling, or in the provision of services or facilities in connection with such dwelling, because of a handicap of
  - that buyer or renter;
  - a person residing in or intending to reside in that dwelling after it is so sold, rented, or made available; or
  - any person associated with that buyer or renter.

Note: The Fair Housing Act's requirements regarding reasonable modifications and reasonable accommodations are covered in Chapter 3, Fair Housing In Property Management.

Group Homes

The Fair Housing Act's prohibitions against handicap discrimination were clearly intended to curb land use restrictions on group homes for handicapped persons. The Congress that passed the 1988 Amendments Act was aware of cases where state and local governments used their laws and regulations to discriminate against nonrelated disabled individuals seeking to live in congregate arrangements. The House Judiciary Committee report explicitly stated that the 1988 act is intended to apply to "state or local land use and health and safety laws, regulations, practices or decisions which discriminate against individuals with handicaps."

Congress also recognized that group homes could also be blocked by private restrictive covenants and further that neutral rules could indeed have a discriminatory impact on handicapped persons.

Supreme Court Rules City's Occupancy Limit Not Exempt From the Fair Housing Act—City of Edmonds v. Oxford House, Inc. (No. 9423, 1995 US Lexis 3181) U.S. Supreme Court

In what has been hailed as a major victory for group-home providers, the U.S. Supreme Court ruled that the Fair Housing Act's exemption for reasonable local or state occupancy restrictions does not cover rules designed to preserve the family character of a neighborhood, just overcrowding. Oxford House was a group home for 10 to 12 recovering alcoholics and drug abusers located in Edmonds, Washington. An Edmonds zoning ordinance defined a family as no more than five unrelated persons.

The city issued criminal citations charging that Oxford House had violated the zoning ordinance. Oxford House and the Department of Justice countersued, alleging that the city was required to make a reasonable accommodation under the Fair Housing Act by allowing the group home to locate in a single-family residential neighborhood. The district court ruled for the City of Edmonds, but the 9th Circuit reversed.

The case then went to the U.S. Supreme Court, which ruled that the Fair Housing Act's exemption applied only to total occupancy limits that serve to protect against overcrowding. The significance of this decision is that group homes will be free to locate in residential neighborhoods once they have demonstrated that the location is reasonable and necessary to accommodate disabled residents.

New Mexico Supreme Court Rules Enforcement of Restrictive Covenant Violates Fair Housing Act*—Hill v. Community of Damien of Molokai, *121 N.M. 353, 911 P.2d 861 (1996)

A residence in the Four Hills Village subdivision of Albuquerque was leased in December 1992 as a group home for people with AIDS, as well as other terminal illnesses. The nonprofit corporation operating the group home will be referred to as the "Community." The four residents who eventually moved into the Community's group home were unrelated, and each required some degree of in-home nursing care.

The plaintiffs, who will be referred to as the "Neighbors," lived on the same dead-end street as the group home. Shortly after the group home opened, the Neighbors noticed an increase in traffic on their street, going to and from the group home. The Neighbors believed that the Community's use of its house as a group home for people with AIDS violated one of the restrictive covenants applicable to all homes in Four Hills Village that stated, among other things, that "no lot shall ever be used for any purpose other than single family residence purposes."

The Neighbors specifically argued that the term single-family residence does not include group homes in which unrelated people live together. On August 12, 1993, the Neighbors filed for an injunction to enforce the covenant and to prevent further use of the Community's house as a group home.

The trial court held that the restrictive covenant prevented the use of the Community's house as a group home for people with AIDS and issued a permanent injunction against the Community. The Community appealed the trial court's order, and the New Mexico Supreme Court granted a stay of the permanent injunction, pending its appeal.

The New Mexico Supreme Court stated that the group home is designed to provide four individuals who live in the house with a traditional family structure, setting, and atmosphere, and that the individuals who reside there use the home much as any family with a disabled family member would.

The word family is not defined in the restrictive covenant and nothing in the covenant suggests that it applies only to individuals related by blood or by law, and other courts have consistently held that restrictive covenants mandating single-family residences do not bar group homes in which the occupants live as a family unit.

The court cited fair housing law and remarked: "Section 3604(f)(3)(B) states, 'for purposes of this subsection, discrimination includes . . . a refusal to make reasonable accommodations in rules, policies, practices, or services, when such accommodations may be necessary to afford such person equal opportunity to use and enjoy a dwelling.' We conclude that the Fair Housing Act factors weigh in favor of the Community. A covenant that restricts occupancy only to related individuals or that bars group homes has a disparate impact not only on the current residents for the Community's group home who have AIDS but also on all disabled individuals who need congregate living arrangements in order to live in traditional neighborhoods and communities. We find it significant that the trial court rejected the Neighbors' proposed finding of fact that this additional traffic posed any increased safety hazard to the neighborhood. Accordingly, we conclude that the negative effects of increased traffic, without any additional harm, are outweighed by the Community's interest in maintaining its congregate home for individuals with AIDS. Because the Community has proved a 'disparate impact' under FHA, the Neighbors cannot enforce the covenant against the Community. . . ."

Design and Construction Requirements for New Housing

The 1988 Fair Housing Amendments Act requires that all covered multifamily dwellings first occupied after March 13, 1991, be designed and constructed with certain accessibility-enhancing features, including a building entrance on an accessible route. Covered **multifamily dwellings** include buildings consisting of four or more dwelling units, if such buildings have one or more elevators, and ground floor dwelling units in other buildings consisting of four or more dwelling units. On March 6, 1991, HUD published the "Fair Housing Accessibility Guidelines" in the Federal Register to provide technical assistance to builders, developers, and others in the development chain.

Accessibility features. The following features are mandated for new multifamily dwellings:

- Public and common use areas must be "readily accessible to and usable by handicapped persons."
- All doors designed to allow passage into and within all premises must be sufficiently wide to accommodate persons who use wheelchairs.
- There must be an accessible route into and through the dwelling unit.
- Light switches, electrical outlets, thermostats, and other environmental controls must be placed in accessible locations.
- Reinforcements must be installed in bathrooms to allow for the later installation of grab bars.
- Kitchens and bathrooms must be designed to allow people in wheelchairs to maneuver about the space.

AIDS Disclosure

Stigmatized property may include property in which the current or former occupant is infected with the human immunodeficiency virus (HIV) or diagnosed with the acquired immunodeficiency syndrome (AIDS). AIDS is a fatal disease that affects the body's ability to fight infection. AIDS can be transmitted through

- sexual contact;
- inoculation with HIV-infected blood; and
- pregnancy, from an infected mother to her child.

The Centers for Disease Control and Prevention and the surgeon general both stress that AIDS is not transmitted through casual daily contact. You cannot get the virus from the following:

- Toilets
- Doorknobs
- Telephones
- Office machinery
- Household furniture

This is significant for the real estate profession because subsequent occupants of property formerly occupied by persons with AIDS are not at risk of contracting the disease simply by occupying the property.

Prospective purchasers may express concern about possible health risks associated with such a property. These fears are unfounded.

Fair Housing Concerns

The 1988 Fair Housing Amendments Act established persons with handicaps, which includes those diagnosed with AIDS, as a new protected class. It is illegal to discriminate against people with handicaps, just as it is illegal to discriminate on the basis of race, color, religion, sex, national origin, or familial status. The legislative history of the Fair Housing Act makes it clear that Congress intended coverage to include persons suffering from communicable diseases such as AIDS.

According to HUD, it is illegal for real estate agents to make unsolicited disclosures that a current or former occupant of the property has AIDS. If a prospective purchaser directly asks an agent if a current or former occupant has AIDS, and the agent knows this is in fact true, HUD advises that the agent should not respond.

Real estate agents who respond to this question by providing information regarding the AIDS status of a current or former occupant run the risk of violating the fair housing laws. The best response is to tell the purchasers to pursue the investigation on their own if they have determined this information to be relevant to their decision to purchase the property.

Fair Housing Risk Reduction Tips for Buyer's Agents

When a real estate agent is listing a home and the seller directs the agent to exclude certain buyers based on their race, the decision the agent faces is simple—decline the listing. Fair housing law compliance issues are more complex for the buyer's agent. The following are typical questions that buyers ask:

Is this a safe neighborhood?

What are the crime statistics in the area?

Can you tell me about the quality of the schools?

What is the ethnic composition of the neighborhood?

Can you show me homes in a ________ neighborhood?

The best way to answer such questions is to provide purchasers with information about where they can find the information they seek. There is less liability for brokers and sales associates in being the source of the source of the information and not the source itself.

The Americans with Disabilities Act

The Americans with Disabilities Act (ADA) was signed into law on July 26, 1990, by President George H. W. Bush and has been called the most comprehensive civil rights legislation to be enacted in the last quarter century. The purpose of the ADA is to eliminate discrimination directed toward the approximately 43 million individuals with disabilities and allow them to enter the social and economic mainstream of society. This will be accomplished by providing equal opportunities in employment, transportation, access to goods and services offered by both the public and private sector, and communications.

The ADA was not intended to cover housing, and it specifically exempts "facilities that are covered or expressly exempted from coverage under the Fair Housing Act of 1968." However, the ADA could be applied to facilities that operate a "place of public accommodation," which would be covered by Title III, such as the rental office in an apartment complex. Title III mandates that public facilities, goods, and services must be accessible to persons with disabilities. Public accommodations must remove architectural barriers whenever readily achievable; make reasonable changes in policies, practices, and procedures; and provide auxiliary aids or services unless to do so would result in an undue burden, or would pose a direct threat to the health or safety of others.

Sales Office in Model Home Subject to ADA Requirements—Sapp v. MHI P'ship, Ltd., *199 F. Supp. 2d 578 (N.D. Tex. 2002).*

A Texas federal court has considered whether a developer is liable under the Americans with Disabilities Act (ADA) for failing to make a model home that was used as a sales office accessible to individuals suffering from a disability.

Patricia and Pat Sapp (the "Sapps") both suffer from medical conditions that require that they use wheelchairs. The Sapps were interested in building a home in the Plantation Homes housing development. Mrs. Sapp called a sales representative for the developer, and she told Mrs. Sapp to come to a model home that she was using as a sales office. In response to a question from Mrs. Sapp, the salesperson also informed Mrs. Sapp over the telephone that the model home was wheelchair accessible. However, when the Sapps arrived at the model home, they discovered that neither the front nor the back door had a ramp making the model home wheelchair accessible. Although Mrs. Sapp was able to negotiate the front steps while in her wheelchair and obtain the sales information inside the model home, on the way out her wheelchair spilled over and she suffered injuries. The Sapps sued MHI Partnership d/b/a Plantation Homes ("Developer") for violations of the ADA and a Texas statute.

The U.S. District Court, Northern District of Texas, ruled in favor of the Sapps. The purpose of the law is to ensure equal access and services for disabled individuals and requires that a place of public accommodation be "readily accessible and usable by individuals with disabilities." The ADA lists a number of places that constitute places of public accommodation, one of which is "a sales or rental establishment."

The court first determined that the Sapps were disabled, as defined in the ADA, and that the Developer's model home was not accessible to Mrs. Sapp. The only question remaining was whether a model home sales office was subject to the terms of the ADA. The court ruled that because the model home was used as a sales office, it was a place of public accommodation and the ADA applied to it.

The Developer argued that because the model home would be sold and eventually used as a private residence, it was not subject to the ADA. The Developer also argued that because no transactions were closed in the model home, it did not constitute a sales office. The Developer's final argument was that the Sapps could have obtained the information from the Developer's other offices that were accessible as defined by the ADA. The court rejected all arguments and found Developers liable for damages under a Texas statute barring discrimination against individuals with disabilities.

Summary

The 1988 Fair Housing Amendments Act added familial status and handicap as protected classes and greatly strengthened the enforcement mechanisms. HUD regulations, which went into effect March 12, 1989, further defined discriminatory housing practices and gave a great deal of authoritative material concerning the meaning of the Fair Housing Act. The regulations added a provision that covered obtaining property and hazard insurance and prohibited the refusal to provide such insurance outright based on protected class factors or subjecting those individuals to different terms or conditions for obtaining coverage. Both the Fair Housing Act and HUD regulations condemn discriminatory lending practices.

Buyer's agents with an in-depth understanding of fair housing laws will be able to better assist their clients if they encounter discrimination at any point during the home purchasing process, including obtaining financing and property insurance.

case study

Real estate broker Deryk Michaels worked almost exclusively in a 336-unit housing development called Windmill Village. Lynn Ellis lived in the village, and later on her daughter and granddaughter moved in with her. However, Windmill Village did not allow children younger than 16 to live there and evicted Ellis and her family. This happened before the 1988 Fair Housing Amendments Act that added familial status as a protected class.

After the effective date of the amendments, Windmill Village did not allow the family to move back. Michaels complained to HUD regarding business damages associated with the prohibition on children and asserted that Windmill Village did not qualify for the over-55 exemption. Ellis and her daughter also filed complaints with HUD alleging family status discrimination.

After HUD issued a charge, the Department of Justice filed a suit on behalf of both Ellis and Michaels.

1. Do you believe Ellis and her family were victims of housing discrimination? If yes, explain why.
2. Was Michaels a victim of housing discrimination because of his business losses?
3. If you were a member of the jury, what damages, if any, would you award to the complainants?

Chapter 2 Review Questions

1. The 1988 Fair Housing Amendments Act
   a. changed the cap on punitive damage awards to $100,000.
   b. made attorney's fees available to prevailing plaintiffs.
   c. extended the statute of limitations from 180 days to two years for filing a complaint with HUD.
   d. added marital status as a protected class.

2. The 1988 Fair Housing Amendments Act added which of the following two classes?
   a. Marital status and handicap
   b. Marital status and familial status
   c. Age and handicap
   d. Handicap and familial status

3. The Fair Housing Amendments Act of 1988 prohibits housing discrimination against all of the following *EXCEPT*
   a. pregnant women.
   b. families with children younger than 18.
   c. college students.
   d. someone about to obtain custody of a child younger than 18.

4. The court case that ruled that enforcement of restrictive covenants violates the Fair Housing Act was *The City of Edmonds v. Oxford House.*
   a. True
   b. False

5. Which statement is *FALSE* regarding predatory lending?
   a. The loan is not justified by the creditworthiness of the borrower.
   b. The loan is secured by the borrower's home.
   c. The loan includes outrageous terms and conditions.
   d. Predatory lenders do not target elderly women.

6. The Equal Credit Opportunity Act
   a. covers applications for mortgages.
   b. is enforced through HUD.
   c. Both of these
   d. Neither of these

7. In the *City of Edmonds v. Oxford House,* the Supreme Court ruled that
   a. the Fair Housing Act's occupancy standards were designed to preserve the family character of areas.
   b. Oxford House had violated local zoning laws.
   c. a group home's location must be reasonable and necessary to accommodate disabled residents.
   d. the City of Edmonds was not required to make a reasonable accommodation under the Fair Housing Act.

8. The definition of the term *handicap* includes all of the following *EXCEPT*
   a. former drug addicts.
   b. alcoholics.
   c. persons who test positive for HIV infection.
   d. current illegal drug users.

9. HUD has declared it illegal to volunteer information regarding a current or former occupant's disease of AIDS.
   a. True
   b. False

10. Which statement is *FALSE* regarding the Americans with Disabilities Act?
    a. The ADA covers housing.
    b. The ADA exempts from coverage facilities that are covered under the Fair Housing Act.
    c. The ADA would cover the rental office in an apartment complex.
    d. The ADA was signed into law on July 26, 1990, by President George H. W. Bush.

chapter three

Fair Housing in Property Management

learning objectives

After completing this chapter, you will be able to

- illustrate how the courts apply the Fair Housing Act to rentals,
- list factors in determining occupancy standards,
- describe the handicap requirements of the law, and
- list the permissible applicant selection inquiries.

Key Terms

reasonable accommodation
reasonable modification
rent

The Fair Housing Act prohibits discrimination in rentals in the same way as it does in sales. HUD regulations identify specific actions that would violate the law in a rental situation based on protected class factors. Under federal law, it is illegal for landlords to discriminate on the basis of race, color, religion, sex, national origin, familial status, and physical or mental handica. Housing providers should check their state and local laws to determine what other groups may be protected.

Prohibited Conduct

- Refusing to **rent** a dwelling or negotiate for the rental of a dwelling
- Using different provisions in leases relating to rental charges and security deposits
- Imposing different rental charges for a dwelling
- Using different qualification criteria or applications
- Employing different rental approval procedures, such as application fees and credit analysis
- Evicting tenants because of their protected class
- Failing or delaying maintenance or repairs
- Failing to process an offer
- Limiting the use of facilities or services associated with the dwelling
- Representing that a lease provision excludes protected groups
- Limiting information about a rental
- Misrepresentation regarding the availability of a rental
- Employing codes or other devices to segregate applicants or renters
- Restricting or attempting to restrict the choices of a renter
- Discouraging any person from inspecting a dwelling
- Steering

A significant number of fair housing complaints involve discrimination directed at families with children and persons with physical or mental handicaps. This may be because some housing providers may not understand the handicap requirements of the law, including providing reasonable accommodations and modifications. Landlords are allowed to adopt reasonable health and safety rules, but what is reasonable can also be subject to challenge, especially if overly restrictive toward children. One landlord required all children age 17 and younger to be accompanied by an adult when using the swimming pool. The judge in that case found the age restriction to be completely ridiculous.

When working with disabled tenants, it is important that the landlord not stereotype and make assumptions about the type of housing that would be appropriate for persons with certain disabilities. For instance, a person with a mobility impairment will not necessarily want a ground-floor apartment or a ranch-style home. Views may be important to a visually impaired individual. Always let the prospect set the limits, regardless of disability.

The importance of employing consistent practices, policies, and procedures cannot be overstated. This begins at the application stage and must continue throughout the residency. All rules and regulations established by the landlord must apply equally and fairly to all residents. For instance, charges for late payments and bounced check charges must be applied equally to all residents. Handling repair requests must be done in a systematic fashion. Landlords are not permitted to provide slower or lower-quality maintenance based on membership in a protected group. Notice of lease violations and eviction procedures must be administered consistently. Just remember, a landlord willing to do something for one resident must be willing to do the same for all; for example, a landlord who allows a flexible payment schedule for one tenant must be consistent and do the same for others.

Disorganization or Discrimination?

Leasing agent Larry has gone hunting and no one else in the office knows anything about the rentals he handles. An Asian couple with two children come in to see an apartment Larry has told them about. The receptionist suggests another complex where she knows there is an apartment available. The Asian couple leave, thinking they have been discriminated against.

Another agent in the office, Tim, instructs his assistant not to bother running a credit check on an applicant because he "feels good" about her. Alicia takes a maintenance request from a white resident and promises to have a repair person out later that day. However, when a Hispanic resident calls to say it has been a week since his repair request was made and nothing has been done about it, Alicia explains that she hasn't been able to get anybody out there to fix the problem.

This conduct may have resulted from simple disorganization, but the result will likely be a lawsuit based on alleged discriminatory practices. This company needs to employ systematic procedures and consistent policies in order to avoid liability under fair housing laws.

Rental Transaction Procedures

Once prospective tenants have been greeted, they should be prequalified. Find out the size and price range they want and determine what their wants and needs are.

Show properties they request and point out facilities such as pool, laundry room, and so forth. Discuss neighborhood facilities, such as location of schools or shopping centers.

The Application Process

Every prospect should be given the same application form to fill out. The landlord should describe the tenant selection process to the prospect:

- Explain how applications are evaluated and how tenants are selected.
- Tell prospects the credit check fee, if any, and whether it is refundable.
- Tell prospects the application deposit amount and when the deposit is refundable.
- Tell prospects how long the application process will take.

Ask the prospects to fill out the form and review it on completion to make sure it is filled out correctly and fully.

The Selection Process

The application should be evaluated using established company selection criteria in an objective manner:

- Run a credit report.

- Do a criminal background check (optional).
- Contact the employer or verify the source of income if the applicant is not employed.
- Check with previous landlords to obtain a rental history.

Call the prospects and inform them of acceptance or denial. If denied, provide prospects with objective reasons.

It is important to note that requiring a person to be employed could violate the Fair Housing Act because persons with certain disabilities may not be able to work and might have other sources of income. It is considered discriminatory to use wording in an ad that states "must be employed" for this reason.

Note: The Fair Housing Act does not require that housing be made available to anyone who poses a direct threat to the health or safety of others or whose tenancy would result in substantial physical damage to the property of others.

HUD regulations allow the following applicant selection inquiries, provided these inquiries are made of all applicants, whether or not they have handicaps:

- To determine ability to meet the financial requirements
- To determine whether an applicant is qualified for a dwelling available only to persons with handicaps or to a person with a specific handicap
- To determine whether an applicant is qualified for priority status as a person with a disability
- To determine whether the applicant is a current illegal drug abuser or addicted to a controlled substance
- To inquire whether an applicant has been convicted of the illegal manufacture or distribution of a controlled substance

Participation in the Section 8 Program

The Housing and Community Development Act of 1974 created a new set of housing assistance programs for lower-income families, the so-called Section 8 programs. Apartment owners, as well as owners of single-family dwellings, who participate in the Section 8 rental programs are prohibited from discriminating against prospective tenants because of their status as holders of Section 8 certificates or vouchers. However, private participation in the programs is not mandatory, and landlords are free to choose whether they want to accept Section 8 tenants.

Landlord May Refuse to Rent to Disabled Section 8 Tenants—Not Violation of U.S. Housing Act or Fair Housing Act. Salute v. Stratford Greens Garden Apartments, *136 F.3d 293 (2d Cir. N.Y. 1998)*

This case involves two disabled individuals who receive Section 8 housing assistance from the federal government. Under the Section 8 program, tenants pay rent of up to 30 percent of their income and the government contracts with the private landlord to pay the rest of the market rent. Participation in the Section 8 program is voluntary on the landlord's part, and a landlord lawfully may refuse to accept rental applications from Section 8 tenants.

In Salute, the plaintiffs wanted to live in the Stratford Greens Garden Apartments (the "Landlord") in Suffolk County, New York. The Landlord's policy was that he will not accept applications from prospective tenants who are Section 8 participants. However, on several past occasions, the Landlord agreed to accept Section 8 payments for tenants already living at the property. Because of their Section 8 participation, both of the plaintiffs were turned down for housing at Stratford Greens. They sued, claiming that the Landlord discriminated against them because of their disabilities by refusing to make "reasonable accommodations" in violation of the federal Fair Housing Act. They also claimed the Landlord had violated the Section 8 "take one, take all" provision of the United States Housing Act.

Ruling for the Landlord, the district court held that there is an exception to the "take one, take all" requirement of the Housing Act where, as here, the only Section 8 tenants are existing tenants who became Section 8 participants while already tenants. The district court also ruled in favor of the Landlord on the FHA claim. The plaintiffs appealed. Before the appeal was heard, Congress repealed the "take one, take all" provision of the Housing Act.

The U.S. Court of Appeals, Second Circuit, upheld the lower court's decision as far as the exception to the "take one, take all" requirement, pointing out that to hold otherwise would punish landlords who, as here, chose not to evict tenants who became Section 8 participants during their tenancy. As for the plaintiffs' claims under the FHA, the court first addressed the issue of whether Section 8 participation was a reasonable accommodation required under the FHA. Stating that "the burdens of Section 8 participation are substantial enough that participation should not be forced on landlords, either as an accommodation to handicap or otherwise," the court held that Section 8 participation constituted 'unreasonable costs,' an 'undue hardship,' and a 'substantial burden,'" which are not required under the FHA's reasonable accommodation provision.

The court then tackled the more basic question: regardless of its reasonableness, whether a landlord's participation in the Section 8 program should be considered an "accommodation" under the FHA. In Salute, the plaintiffs argued that their handicaps created their poor economic status and that they therefore were entitled to an accommodation (the Landlord's participation in the Section 8 program) to remedy their financial situation. The court specifically stated that the FHA addresses "the accommodation of handicaps, not the alleviation of economic disadvantages that may be correlated with having handicaps."

Discrimination toward Families with Children

After March 12, 1989, housing providers could no longer refuse to deal with people because their households included children. Housing providers may not segregate families with children in certain areas of a housing complex any more than racial minorities may be restricted this way.

In addition to forbidding outright refusals to deal, the law requires nondiscriminatory treatment of family tenants. Thus, landlords may not impose higher security deposits or rental charges on families with children.

Case law developed rapidly regarding familial status discrimination in both federal district court and in HUD administrative proceedings after the passage of the 1988 Amendments Act. A record $2.4 million was awarded in 1992 by a Washington, D.C., jury against a large management company for "pattern and practice" discrimination against families with children. The plaintiff was twice turned down for an apartment because she had a child. A HUD administrative law judge rejected a landlord's assertions of health and safety concerns as defenses to claims of family status discrimination after he refused to rent an apartment at the top of steep stairs to a family with children. The significance of this decision is that there is nothing in the Fair Housing Act that will permit housing providers to consider risks and circumstances of a dwelling unit in making rental decisions.

Another landlord was found to have violated the act by honoring a dying resident's request to exclude families with children from the vacant apartment next door. Although the conduct at issue was in no way malicious, the landlord was found guilty of discrimination based on family status.

Fair Plaza Associates Settles Lawsuit with Justice Department for $120,000 Based on Familial Status Discrimination

Fair Plaza Associates, owners of several rental properties in Albuquerque, New Mexico, agreed to pay $120,000 to settle a lawsuit filed against the company by the Department of Justice in September 2002, after an investigation revealed a "pattern" of illegal discriminatory practices. The initial investigation, launched in spring 2000 after complaints were filed by a father and son and a biracial couple, revealed a "pattern and practice" of illegal discriminatory treatment against African Americans and families with children.

One of the complainants, Bill Maher, applied to live at the El Pueblo Apartments in April 2000. The manager told him that she would have to check, but she didn't think they allowed children. Maher contacted the owner of the property who told him in a loud, gruff voice, "No, I don't rent to children, and you can go to Legal Aid for all I care." Maher found that to be very good advice.

The company also had to undergo training in fair housing law as part of the settlement.

Developing Reasonable Occupancy Standards

The Fair Housing Act allows housing providers to adhere to any reasonable local, state, or federal restrictions regarding the maximum number of persons permitted to occupy a dwelling. HUD regulations also permit landlords to develop and implement reasonable occupancy requirements on their own. Although HUD refused to issue "model occupancy standards," the agency does have a rule of thumb that, generally, two persons per bedroom is considered reasonable. The reasonableness will, however, be judged on a case-by-case basis.

Occupancy standards exist to

- protect tenants from unsafe and unhealthy conditions,
- avoid overcrowding, and
- protect physical assets.

Developing Reasonable Occupancy Standards

- State and local fair housing laws
- Size of the bedroom or unit
- Age of the children
- Number of bedrooms and their dimensions
- Configuration of the unit (a bedroom is not considered a bedroom if a person has to pass through another bedroom to access it)
- Physical limitations of the housing
- State and local laws, such as zoning laws
- Capacities of the building, such as sewer and septic systems

When reviewing cases, HUD will also consider the size of the bedrooms and dwelling, the ages of the children, any discriminatory statements, steps taken to discourage families with children, any discriminatory advertising, and other relevant factors such as enforcing occupancy policies only against families with children.

The Building Owners and Code Administrators (BOCA) has issued guidelines concerning minimum occupancy area requirements in square feet. BOCA requires a minimum of 150 square feet for the first occupant and an additional 100 square feet for each additional person. Sleeping areas must have 70 square feet for a single occupant. In situations where two or more people share sleeping space, BOCA requires a minimum of 50 square feet per person. In computing total square footage of a dwelling, BOCA includes only living and dining rooms, kitchens, and bedrooms.

BOCA defines an occupant as "any individual beyond one year of age, living and sleeping in a dwelling unit, or having actual possession of said dwelling or rooming unit."

In developing occupancy policies, housing providers should always ask, "Could three people live in this one-bedroom unit?" or "Could five people live in this two-bedroom dwelling?"

The first appellate court decision involving occupancy standards in a family status discrimination case was *U.S. v. Badgett.* The court cited HUD's rule of thumb that an occupancy policy of two persons per bedroom is presumptively reasonable in determining that the defendant had violated the Fair Housing Act by refusing to rent a one-bedroom apartment to a single mother and her five-year-old daughter. The manager offered to rent them either a two-bedroom or a three-bedroom apartment at a significantly higher rent. The apartment complex had been an "all adult" complex before the passage of the 1988 Fair Housing Amendments Act and did not qualify for exempted status as housing for older persons.

$250,000 Settlement Reached in Virginia Occupancy Limit Lawsuit—Fair Housing Council of Greater Washington v. West Group Inc., *No. 951262A*

A Virginia apartment complex reached a $250,000 settlement of a lawsuit alleging that its occupancy limit of no more than three people in a two-bedroom apartment violated the Fair Housing Act. The complex refused to rent a two-bedroom unit to two women and their two small children. The women were told they would have to rent a three-bedroom apartment at a higher monthly rent. Testing confirmed that complex prohibited four persons from occupying a two-bedroom apartment. The lawsuit stated that the occupancy policy was unreasonable and had an adverse effect on families with children, in violation of the Fair Housing Act. A 1991 HUD policy memo stated that a two-person-per-bedroom occupancy standard is presumptively reasonable under the Fair Housing Act.

Developing Reasonable Health and Safety Rules

Housing providers are entitled to develop and implement reasonable health and safety rules relating to the use of their dwellings and the facilities associated with them. HUD regulations recognize that such rules may be appropriate in situations where landlords and property managers believe their dwellings or facilities may pose special risks for tenants and want to avoid potential liability for injuries caused by such risks.

One way a landlord may prohibit unwanted behavior is to make rules that are age-neutral. For instance, a landlord who desires to prevent certain conduct in the laundry room, such as loud behavior and water fights, can have rules prohibiting any person, child or otherwise, from such conduct.

Court Rulings Regarding Reasonable Health and Safety Rules

- Rule excluding children from utility rooms unless accompanied by an adult not illegal—*HUD v. Guglielmi*
- Rule restricting children of a certain age from using swimming pool and other recreational facilities without an accompanying adult serve legitimate safety and maintenance purposes—*HUD v. Murphy*

Landlord's Rules Discriminate Against Families with Children—Fair Housing Congress v. Weber, *993 F. Supp. 1286 (E.D. Mo. 1998)*

A decision from a federal district court in California provides an in-depth analysis of Section 804 of the Fair Housing Act (the "FHA"). This case involved a 26-unit apartment complex (the "Property") located in Torrence, California. Former tenants who had small children and a fair housing organization sued the manager and the owners of the Property, claiming that some of the rules, formal and informal, violated the FHA by discriminating against families with children. Some of the apartments have their entrances on the ground level, but the bulk of the units have second-floor entrances.

Rule 8 of the Property's "Pool and Building Rules" states in part: "Children will not be allowed to play or run around inside the building area at any time because of disturbance to other tenants or damage to building property. Bikes, carriages, strollers, tricycles, wagons, etc., must be kept inside apartments or in garage area and not left outside. . . ."

The property manager, who had experienced a dangerous situation involving another former tenant, also had an informal rule that she would not rent any units with second-floor entrances to families with small children, and she communicated this rule to prospective tenants.

The Fair Housing Act prohibits advertising that indicates any preference, limitation, or discrimination based on familial status, as well as discriminatory terms, conditions, and privileges of a rental dwelling because of familial status.

The court easily found that the first sentence of the Property's Rule 8 clearly was a restriction on the use of apartment facilities by tenant children, and because it discriminated against tenants with children on the basis of their familial status, it violated the Fair Housing Act. The second sentence of Rule 8, unlike the first sentence, was not discriminatory on its face. There was no evidence that it indicated any preference, limitation, or discrimination based on familial status, so the court found that it did not violate the Fair Housing Act.

The plaintiffs also charged that the property manager's practice of steering families with small children away from apartments with second-floor entrances violated the FHA. As the court explained, "'Steering' is not an outright refusal to rent to a person within a class of people protected by the statute; rather it consists of efforts to deprive a protected homeseeker of housing opportunities in certain locations." So, even if the property manager's preference not to have families with small children occupy the second-floor entry units is based on legitimate safety concerns, her informal rule nonetheless violated the Fair Housing Act.

In addition, even though the owners of the Property did not participate in the actual discriminatory practices, as the court pointed out, the duty imposed by the FHA not to discriminate may not be delegated, and "a property owner is liable for the discriminatory acts of employees even if the property owner instructed his employees not to discriminate."

It is important to note that these cases involve reasonable health and safety rules. Several courts have articulated that there is nothing in the Fair Housing Act that permits the owner to determine that risks and circumstances of his dwelling or neighborhood make it inappropriate for children. That decision is for the tenant. Refer to the earlier case involving the landlord who refused to rent an apartment at the top of steep stairs to a family with children.

Discrimination Based on Disability

Housing providers may not inquire whether a person has a disability or into the nature or severity of a disability, unless it is necessary to qualify a person for a special government housing unit. A housing provider may ask a handicapped person to provide evidence that supports the need for the accommodation after a request for an accommodation has been made.

Reasonable Modifications

The Fair Housing Act requires that persons with disabilities be allowed, at their own expense, to make **reasonable modifications** necessary for their full and equal enjoyment of the dwelling. A housing provider's refusal to permit the modifications as required by the law amounts to discrimination based on handicap. Examples of modifications include widening doorways, installing grab bars, and lowering kitchen cabinets. The premises to which these modifications may be made are not limited to the interior of the handicapped person's unit but also include lobbies, main entrances, and other public and common use areas of a building.

Note: Landlords may, if they desire, keep the unit with the accessibility features in place and advertise the unit as "handicap accessible" without violating the Fair Housing Act's prohibition of discriminatory advertising.

In a case involving a rental, a landlord may, where it is reasonable to do so, condition permission for a modification on the renter's agreeing to restore the interior of the premises to the condition that existed before the modification, reasonable wear and tear excepted. The restoration requirement may be imposed only on modifications made to the interior areas of an individual unit, not on those made to public or common areas. It would not be considered reasonable, however, to insist that widened doorways be made narrow again. On the other hand, landlords would be able to require that grab bars be removed or that lowered kitchen cabinets be restored to their original height.

Landlords may not increase any customarily required security deposits for handicapped persons, but they are permitted to negotiate a provision in the restoration agreement requiring that the tenant pay into an interest-bearing escrow account, over a reasonable period of time, a reasonable amount of money to fund the restoration. The interest must accrue to the benefit of the tenant. A landlord may also condition permission for a modification on the renter's providing a reasonable description of the proposed modifications, as well as reasonable assurances that the work will be done in a workmanlike manner and that any required building permits will be obtained.

Reasonable Accommodations

The Fair Housing Act requires that housing providers make **reasonable accommodations** in rules, policies, practices, or services, when such accommodations are necessary to afford a handicapped person equal opportunity to use and enjoy a dwelling unit. The concept of reasonable accommodations is derived from regulations and case law interpreting the Rehabilitation Act of 1973. An accommodation that permits handicapped tenants to experience the full benefit of tenancy must be made unless the accommodation imposes an undue financial or administrative burden or requires a fundamental alteration in the nature of its program.

Examples of reasonable accommodations include allowing a person with a visual impairment to have an assistive animal in a building that has a no-pets policy and allowing a person with a mobility impairment to have a reserved parking space near the apartment, even though the complex does not have assigned parking. Another example would be to allow nonresidents the use of the laundry room so they may assist a disabled resident. Residents may even have "emotional support pets" that provide needed support and, in some cases, provide other assistance. Dogs have been trained to sense an epileptic seizure before it happens, break the owner's fall when one occurs, and even dial 911.

New HUD Guidance Regarding Assistance Animals

On October 27, 2008, HUD issued a final rule amending the requirements for pet ownership in HUD-assisted public housing and multifamily housing projects for the elderly and persons with disabilities. The final rule conforms these pet ownership requirements to the requirements for animals assisting persons with disabilities in HUD's other public housing programs. Both regulations now provide that pet rules do not apply to animals that "assist, support, or provide service to persons with disabilities."

While these regulations address public housing, the rule provides vital guidance on HUD's fair housing enforcement stance on assistance animals. The final rule does not change existing HUD policy, which applies the Fair Housing Act and Section 504 of the Rehabilitation Act reasonable accommodation principles. The most substantive change made by the final rule is the removal of animal training and tenant certification requirements.

Key in the new rule is the removal of the requirement that the tenant certify in writing that the animal has been trained to assist with a specific disability.

Certain animals provide assistance or perform tasks and services for persons with disabilities. Such animals are often called service animals, assistance animals, support animals, therapy animals, companion animals, and emotional support animals.

Under both the Fair Housing Act and Section 504, in order for a requested accommodation to qualify as a reasonable accommodation, the requester must have a disability, and the accommodation must be necessary to afford a person with a disability an equal opportunity to use and enjoy the dwelling unit. To show that a requested accommodation may be necessary, there must be an identifiable relationship, or nexus, between the requested accommodation and the person's disability. The requester must also demonstrate a nexus between the disability and the function the service animal provides.

Examples of disability-related functions include the following:

- Guiding individuals who are blind or have low vision
- Alerting individuals who are deaf or hard of hearing to sounds
- Providing protection or rescue assistance
- Pulling a wheelchair
- Fetching items
- Alerting persons to impending seizures
- Providing emotional support to persons with disabilities who have a disability-related need for such support

Housing providers are entitled to verify the existence of the disability and the need for an accommodation if either is not readily apparent. If a request is made to have an emotional support animal, a landlord can request documentation from a physician, psychiatrist, social worker, or other mental health professional that the animal alleviates at least one identifiable symptom of the person's disability.

Housing providers are not required to provide any accommodations that would

- pose a direct threat to the health or safety of others;
- result in substantial physical damage to the property of others, unless the threat can be eliminated or significantly reduced by a reasonable accommodation;
- pose an undue financial or administrative burden; or
- fundamentally alter the nature of the provider's operations.

A request for an assistance animal can be denied when the animal's behavior poses a direct threat and the owner takes no effective action to control the behavior. Determination of the threat must be an individualized assessment about the specific animal, such as its current conduct or recent past history. The assessment must consider the nature, duration, or severity of the risk of injury, as well as the probability that potential injury will actually occur and whether reasonable modifications of rules, policies, practices, or procedures will reduce the risk. Actions by the owner to reduce the risk include obtaining specific training, medication, or equipment for the animal.

If a housing provider's insurance carrier would cancel or substantially increase the costs of the policy because of the presence of a certain breed of dog, HUD will find that this poses an undue financial or administrative burden. An investigator must substantiate the housing provider's claim by verifying such a claim directly with the insurance company and considering whether comparable insurance, without the restriction, is available in the marketplace. If the investigator finds evidence that the insurance company has a policy of refusing to insure all properties with animals without regard to assistance animals in violation of the Fair Housing Act, it may refer the information to the Department of Justice for investigation.

A person with a disability who uses an assistance animal is responsible for the animal's care and maintenance. A housing provider may establish rules in the lease agreement requiring a person with a disability to pick up and dispose of the assistance animal's waste.

A housing provider may not require an applicant to pay a fee or a security deposit as a condition of allowing the applicant to keep an assistance animal. However, if the assistance animal causes any damage to the dwelling unit or the common use areas, the landlord may require the tenant to pay the repair costs or deduct the charges from the standard security deposit imposed on all tenants.

Colorado Landlord Must Attempt to Accommodate Mentally Ill Tenant Prior to Eviction—Roe v. Housing Authority of Boulder *(No. 94-B-2 033, 1995)*

Before evicting a 79-year-old mentally ill tenant as a threat to the health and safety of others, a Colorado landlord must attempt to make a reasonable accommodation for the tenant's mental illness, a federal district judge ruled. Roe, a Boulder resident, had a long history of mental illness and a hearing impairment. The complaints about Roe included allegations that he struck and injured another resident and threatened the property manager. After the housing authority initiated eviction proceedings, Roe sued the authority and the City of Boulder, claiming discrimination under the Fair Housing Act. Roe charged that the housing authority had failed to reasonably accommodate his mental disability and that his aggressive behavior was related to his disability. The judge agreed with Roe and ruled that he could not be evicted until the authority could demonstrate that no reasonable accommodation would eliminate or acceptably minimize any risk Roe posed to other residents.

■ Summary

Today's real estate professional, acting in the capacity of a property manager, faces significant fair housing law compliance challenges. That is because there are vast opportunities to violate the law, and often the licensee is not even aware that discriminatory conduct is occurring. The name of the game is consistency, consistency, consistency. At all times, both prospects and residents must receive equal treatment under the law.

As in the case of a seller who attempts to act in an illegal manner under the Fair Housing Act, the owner of rental property might also direct the licensee to discriminate against persons protected by the law. In my own property management practice, I have been instructed to exclude families with children because of noise and damage concerns. If, after explaining the requirements of the Fair Housing Act, the property owner is still reluctant to abide by the law, the real estate professional must refrain from entering into a management contract. It is a good idea to have language in the management agreement indicating a commitment to equal opportunity and that the property will be made available to all persons without regard to race, color, religion, sex, national origin, familial status, physical or mental handicap, or membership in any other group protected by local or state law.

case study

Katy and Kyle Dalton owned a home situated on a rocky ocean cliff with a manufactured deck ten feet above ground. Ms. Dalton was a concert pianist. They actually lived in the house during the summer months and rented it out for the remaining nine months. The Daltons contracted with real estate agent Christine Russell to find suitable renters.

Antonio and Robin Maez and their three children, 10-year-old Brooke, a very active 4-year-old named Brandon, and 18-month-old Brayanah, tried to rent the property. Based on safety fears regarding the children, the Maez family was rejected. The Daltons were also concerned for their prized possessions.

Antonio and Robin Maez filed a complaint alleging housing discrimination based on their familial status.

1. Do you think a discriminatory act occurred? Why or why not?
2. Can health and safety concerns be the basis of refusing to rent to a family with children?
3. If the Daltons had not hired agent Christine Russell to represent them, would they have been exempt from the Fair Housing Act?
4. What would have happened if the Daltons had rented out their house and placed an ad stating "No Children"?

Chapter 3 Review Questions

1. A property manager may
   a. require an additional deposit for families with children.
   b. run a credit check on the applicant.
   c. require that a person seeking to rent a dwelling be employed.
   d. restrict families with children to ground-floor units.

2. Which statement is *FALSE* regarding a landlord's health and safety rules?
   a. The rules may be age neutral.
   b. They may apply to all residents.
   c. The rules may be overly restrictive toward families with children.
   d. They may require that children younger than a certain age be accompanied by an adult to use the pool.

3. Participation in the Section 8 assistance program is mandatory.
   a. True
   b. False

4. A property manager may
   a. require that all assistive animals complete special training.
   b. require a special deposit for an assistive animal.
   c. charge a deposit to restore the unit after modifications are made.
   d. inquire about the nature and extent of a person's disability.

5. In developing reasonable occupancy standards, a housing provider may consider all of the following *EXCEPT*
   a. capacities of the building.
   b. size of the unit.
   c. the lack of playground facilities.
   d. zoning laws.

6. Occupancy standards exist to
   a. preserve the family character of a neighborhood.
   b. prevent overcrowding.
   c. both of these
   d. neither of these

7. In reviewing complaints based on occupancy policies, HUD will consider all of the following *EXCEPT*
   a. physical limitations of the housing.
   b. number of bedrooms and their dimensions.
   c. whether an adult and a child will share a bedroom.
   d. configuration of the unit.

8. The definition of the term *handicap* includes all of the following *EXCEPT*
   a. former drug addicts.
   b. alcoholics.
   c. persons who test positive for HIV infection.
   d. current illegal drug users.

9. The Fair Housing Act permits landlords to do all of the following *EXCEPT*
   a. inquire whether an applicant is a current illegal drug user.
   b. ask an applicant about the nature or severity of a disability.
   c. ask applicants whether they can meet the financial requirements of tenancy.
   d. inquire whether an applicant has been convicted of a drug-related felony.

10. Which statement is *TRUE* regarding modifications made to existing dwelling units, as required by the Fair Housing Act?
   a. A landlord may withhold permission for the modification without violating the law.
   b. A landlord must allow the tenant to make any modifications requested.
   c. A landlord may negotiate that money be escrowed over a reasonable period to restore the dwelling.
   d. A landlord may not require a description of the work to be performed.

Fair Housing Advertising

learning objectives

After completing this chapter, you will be able to

- discuss the Fair Housing Act's prohibition of discriminatory advertising,
- list the potential defendants in a fair housing advertising complaint,
- recognize words and phrases that violate the Fair Housing Act, and
- create protected class–sensitive advertising.

Key Terms

catchwords

HUD Publisher's Notice

ordinary reader

Section 804(C) of the Fair Housing Act makes it unlawful "to make, print, or publish, or cause to be made, printed, or published, any notice, statement, or advertisement, with respect to the sale or rental of a dwelling, that indicates any preference, limitation, or discrimination because of race, color, religion, sex, handicap, familial status, or national origin, or an intention to make such preference, limitation, or discrimination."

This prohibition applies to all advertising media, including newspapers, magazines, television, radio, and the Internet. HUD has found newspapers in violation of the Fair Housing Act for publishing discriminatory advertisements and therefore has concluded that it is illegal for Web sites to publish discriminatory advertisements as well. In order to ensure that Web sites do not provide an open market for unlawful discriminatory conduct, HUD continues to investigate allegations that Web sites have published discriminatory advertisements on the Internet.

The *Hunter* Case

It is important to note that a homeowner or a landlord whose dwelling is exempt from coverage under the Fair Housing Act is not free to employ discriminatory advertising. In 1972, the court of appeals noted in *United States v. Hunter* that though free to indulge their discriminatory preferences in selling or renting that dwelling, housing providers do not have the right to publicize that intent to discriminate. The *Hunter* decision was significant because it established judicial guidelines with respect to understanding the meaning of the Fair Housing Act's prohibited practices concerning discriminatory advertising. The *Hunter* opinion also established three important points about Section 804(C):

- That it applies to newspapers and other media
- That the provision does not violate the First Amendment's guarantee of freedom of the press
- That whether or not an advertisement violates the act will be determined by how an **ordinary reader** would interpret the ad

The antidiscriminatory mandate of this provision has a significant impact on the housing industry because it outlaws virtually every discriminatory notice, statement, and advertisement that relates to a housing transaction. Thus, statements made by housing providers that attempt to either encourage or discourage homeseekers from buying or renting in a particular building or neighborhood because of membership in a protected class would violate the law. For example, statements indicating that blacks are not welcome or would not be compatible with existing tenants would be prohibited. The practice of steering homeseekers to certain areas, as well as any discriminatory language contained in restrictive covenants in deeds, would violate the Fair Housing Act.

HUD Advertising Guidelines

In 1989, HUD published advertising guidelines (Appendix I to Part 109, Fair Housing Advertising), which detail the types of advertising prohibited by the Fair Housing Act. The purpose of the HUD guidelines is to assist all advertising media, advertising agencies, and all other persons who use advertising to make, print, or publish or cause to be made, printed, or published advertisements with respect to the sale, rental, or financing of dwellings that are in compliance with the requirements of the Fair Housing Act. HUD published additional guidelines in 1995, which were based on a group of key words determined by HUD to not be discriminatory.

The guidelines also describe the matters that HUD will review in evaluating compliance with the Fair Housing Act in connection with investigations of complaints alleging discriminatory housing practices involving advertising.

The HUD advertising guidelines categorize discriminatory advertising into three groups: (1) advertising that contains words, phrases, symbols, or visual aids that indicate a discriminatory preference or limitation; (2) advertising that selectively uses media, human models, logos, and locations to indicate an illegal preference or limitation; and (3) various types of discriminatory advertising practices condemned by the Fair Housing Act.

Use of Words, Phrases, Symbols, and Visual Aids

HUD regulations prohibit the use of **catchwords,** phrases, symbols, photographs, and illustrations that convey that dwellings are available or not available to a particular group of persons because of race, color, religion, sex, handicap, familial status, or national origin. The words, phrases, and symbols in the following list typify those most often used in residential real estate advertising to convey either overt or tacit discriminatory preferences or limitations:

- Words descriptive of dwelling, landlord, and tenants: *white private home, colored home, Jewish home, Hispanic residence, adult building*
- Words indicative of race, color, religion, sex, handicap, familial status, or national origin
  - Race: *African American, Caucasian, American Indian*
  - Color: *White, black*
  - Religion: *Protestant, Christian, Catholic, Jewish*
  - National origin: *Mexican American, Puerto Rican, Philippine, Polish, Hungarian, Irish, Italian, African, Hispanic, Chinese, Indian, Latino*
  - Sex: The exclusive use of words in advertisements, including those involving the rental of separate units in a single or multifamily dwelling, stating or tending to imply that the housing being advertised is available to persons of only one sex and not the other, except where the sharing of living areas is involved. This section does not cover advertisements of dwellings used exclusively for dormitory facilities by educational institutions.
  - Handicap: *Blind, deaf, mentally ill, impaired, handicapped, physically fit.* This section does not restrict the inclusion of information about the availability of accessible housing.
  - Familial status: *Adults, children, singles, mature persons.* This section does not restrict advertisements of dwellings that are intended and operated for occupancy by older persons and that constitute "housing for older persons."
  - Catchwords: Words and phrases used in a discriminatory context should be avoided, for example, *restricted, exclusive, private, integrated, traditional, board approval,* or *membership approval.*
- Symbols or logotypes that imply or suggest race, color, religion, sex, handicap, familial status, or national origin
- Colloquialisms: Words or phrases used regionally or locally that imply or suggest race, color, religion, sex, handicap, familial status, or national origin
- Directions to real estate for sale or rent (use of maps or written instructions). Directions can imply a discriminatory preference, limitation, or exclusion; for example, references to a real estate location made in terms of landmarks that have racial or national origin significance, such as an existing black development or an existing development known for its exclusion of minorities. References to a synagogue, congregation, or parish may also indicate a religious preference.
- Area description: Names of facilities that cater to a particular racial, national origin, or religious group, such as a country club or private school designations, or names of facilities that are used exclusively by one sex may indicate a preference

Selective Use of Advertising Media or Content

The second general category of unlawful advertising identified in HUD regulations involves the selective use of content or media based on race or other prohibited basis. For example, the selective use of human models in advertisements may have a discriminatory impact. Other examples of this type of discriminatory advertising include the following:

- Selective geographic advertisements: This may involve the strategic placement of billboards, brochure advertisements distributed within a limited geographic area by hand or in the mail, advertising in particular geographic coverage editions of major metropolitan newspapers or in newspapers of limited circulation that are mainly advertising vehicles for reaching a particular segment of the community, or displays or announcements available only in selected sales offices.
- Selective use of equal opportunity slogan or logo: This may involve placing the equal opportunity slogan or logo in advertising reaching some geographic areas but not others, or with respect to some properties but not others.
- Selective use of human models: This regulation covers selective advertising based not only on race but on all of the Fair Housing Act's prohibited bases of discrimination, including sex, handicap, and familial status. The regulations require that human models used in display advertising should be clearly definable as reasonably representing majority and minority groups, both sexes, and, when appropriate, families with children. In addition, models should portray persons in an equal social setting and indicate to the public that the housing is open to all persons, without regard to race, color, religion, sex, handicap, familial status, or national origin.

1995 HUD Memorandum

In January 1995, HUD issued a memorandum on advertising terminology with the purpose of establishing procedures for investigating allegations of discriminatory advertising. The memorandum does not address fair housing issues associated with the publication of advertisements containing human models and does not address liability under the Fair Housing Act for making discriminatory statements.

- Race, color, national origin: Racially neutral terms such as *master bedroom, rare find,* and *desirable neighborhood* will not create liability. However, an ad stating "white family home" or "no Irish" would be illegal.
- Religion: Ads that use the legal name of a religious entity or contain a religious symbol, standing alone, may indicate an illegal preference. But if the ads contain a nondiscrimination disclaimer, the act will not be violated. Advertisements containing descriptions of properties, such as "apartment complex with chapel," do not on their face state a preference for persons likely to make use of those facilities and are not violations of the act.
- Sex: The terms *mother-in-law suite* or *bachelor apartment* will not discriminate on the basis of sex because they are commonly used as physical descriptions of housing units. Use of the term *master bedroom* does not constitute a violation of either the sex or race discrimination provisions of the act.
- Handicap: Advertisers may use descriptive terms such as *great view, walk-in closet,* and *walk to bus stop* without violating the act. Advertising terms related to the conduct required of residents, such as *non-smoking* or *sober,* do not vio-

late the act. Advertisements containing descriptions of accessibility features are lawful, for instance, *wheelchair ramp.*

- Familial status: Advertisers may not limit the number or ages of children but may use terms to describe the property or services and facilities, such as *two bedroom, no bicycles allowed, family room,* or *quiet streets.*

Other Types of Discriminatory Advertising

HUD regulations prohibit the practice of refusing to publish advertisements for the sale or rental of dwellings because of race or other prohibited bases. Such advertisements may not be subject to different charges or terms.

According to the HUD guidelines, all advertising of residential real estate for sale or rent should contain an equal housing opportunity logotype, statement, or slogan (*see* Fig. 4.1) as a means of educating the homeseeking public that the property is available to all persons, regardless of race, color, religion, sex, handicap, familial status, or national origin. The choice of logotype, statement, or slogan will depend on the type of media used and, in space advertising, on the size of the advertisement.

Note:

HUD has published tables to serve as a guide with respect to the size of the logotype in display advertising. At no time should the size of the logotype be smaller than ½ inch by ½ inch in size, and it is not required in advertising of less than four column inches. In any other advertisements, if other logotypes are used, then the Equal Housing Opportunity logo should be of a size at least equal to the largest of the other logotypes. Alternatively, when no other logotypes are used, 3 to 5 percent of an advertisement may be devoted to an equal housing opportunity statement.

The equal housing opportunity statement is as follows:

"We are pledged to the letter and spirit of U.S. Policy for the achievement of EQUAL HOUSING OPPORTUNITY throughout the Nation. We encourage and support an affirmative advertising and marketing program in which there are no barriers to obtaining housing because of race, color, religion, sex, handicap, familial status, or national origin."

Figure 4.1 | The Equal Housing Opportunity Logotype and Slogan

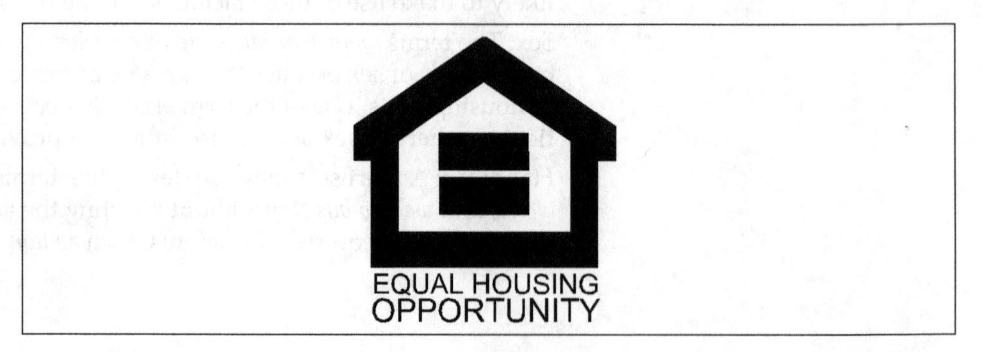

HUD Publisher's Notice

All publishers should publish at the beginning of the real estate advertising section the **HUD Publisher's Notice**, a notice that all the real estate advertised therein is subject to the federal Fair Housing Act, which makes it illegal to advertise any preference, limitation, or discrimination because of race, color, religion, sex, handicap, familial status, or national origin. The notice should state that the publisher will not knowingly accept any advertising for real estate that violates the law. All persons are thereby informed that all dwellings advertised are available on an equal opportunity basis.

Publishers will not intentionally accept discriminatory ads, because if they do, they may be held liable for violating the Fair Housing Act. The first appellate decision to review the merits of a human models case was handed down in 1991 in *Ragin v. The New York Times Co.*, a case brought by plaintiffs who alleged that the Sunday *New York Times* had a 20-year record of publishing housing ads that featured "thousands of human models of whom virtually none were black," except for those black models who were used to depict service employees or homeseekers interested in units in predominantly black neighborhoods. Given the "ordinary reader" concept, the court ruled that the allegations were sufficient to enable them to prove "that the *Times* has published, and continues to publish, some discriminatory ads."

If a human model ad or any other advertising campaign, such as one using words or phrases that express a preference, limitation, or discrimination, runs afoul of the Fair Housing Act, then the *New York Times* decision makes clear that liability extends to the newspaper publishing it as well as to the advertiser placing it.

The Fair Housing Poster

The Secretary of Housing and Urban Development has established regulations with respect to the display of a fair housing poster (*see* Figure 4.2) by persons subject to Sections 804 through 806 of the Fair Housing Act, 42 USC 3604–3606, as follows.

24 CFR § 110.10 Persons subject.

(a) *Except to the extent that paragraph (b) of this section applies, all persons subject to section 804 of the Act, Discrimination in the Sale or Rental of Housing and Other Prohibited Practices, shall post and maintain a fair housing poster as follows:*

(1) *With respect to a single-family dwelling (not being offered for sale or rental in conjunction with the sale or rental of other dwellings) offered for sale or rental through a real estate broker, agent, salesman, or person in the business of selling or renting dwellings, such person shall post and maintain a fair housing poster at any place of business where the dwelling is offered for sale or rental.*

(2) *With respect to all other dwellings covered by the Act:*

(i) *A fair housing poster shall be posted and maintained at any place of business where the dwelling is offered for sale or rental, and*

(ii) *A fair housing poster shall be posted and maintained at the dwelling, except that with respect to a single-family dwelling being offered for sale or rental in conjunction with the sale or rental of other dwellings, the fair housing poster*

Figure 4.2 | Fair Housing Poster

U. S. Department of Housing and Urban Development

EQUAL HOUSING OPPORTUNITY

We Do Business in Accordance With the Federal Fair Housing Law

(The Fair Housing Amendments Act of 1988)

It is illegal to Discriminate Against Any Person Because of Race, Color, Religion, Sex, Handicap, Familial Status, or National Origin

- In the sale or rental of housing or residential lots
- In advertising the sale or rental of housing
- In the financing of housing
- In the provision of real estate brokerage services
- In the appraisal of housing
- Blockbusting is also illegal

Anyone who feels he or she has been discriminated against may file a complaint of housing discrimination:

1-800-669-9777 (Toll Free)
1-800-927-9275 (TTY)

U.S. Department of Housing and Urban Development
Assistant Secretary for Fair Housing and Equal Opportunity
Washington, D.C. 20410

Previous editions are obsolete

form HUD-928.1 (2/2003)

may be posted and maintained at the model dwellings instead of at each of the individual dwellings.

(3) *With respect to those dwellings to which paragraph (a)(2) of this section applies, the fair housing poster must be posted at the beginning of construction and maintained throughout the period of construction and sale or rental.*

(b) *This part shall not require posting and maintaining a fair housing poster:*

(1) *On vacant land, or*

(2) *At any single-family dwelling, unless such dwelling*

(i) *Is being offered for sale or rental in conjunction with the sale or rental of other dwellings in which circumstances a fair housing poster shall be posted and maintained as specified in paragraph (a)(2)(ii) of this section, or*

(ii) *Is being offered for sale or rental through a real estate broker, agent, salesman, or person in the business of selling or renting dwellings in which circumstances a fair housing poster shall be posted and maintained as specified in paragraph (a) (1) of this section.*

(c) *All persons subject to section 805 of the Act, Discrimination in Residential Real Estate-Related Transactions, shall post and maintain a fair housing poster at all their places of business which participate in the covered activities.*

(d) All persons subject to section 806 of the Act, Discrimination in the Provision of Brokerage Services, shall post and maintain a fair housing poster at all their places of business.

24 CFR § 110.15 Location of posters.

All fair housing posters shall be prominently displayed so as to be readily apparent to all persons seeking housing accommodations or seeking to engage in residential real estate–related transactions or brokerage services as contemplated by sections 804 through 806 of the Act.

24 CFR § 110.20 Availability of posters.

All persons subject to this part may obtain fair housing posters from the Department's regional and area offices. A facsimile may be used if the poster and the lettering are equivalent in size and legibility to the poster available from the Department.

24 CFR § 110.25 Description of posters.

(a) *The fair housing poster shall be 11 inches by 14 inches and shall bear the following legend [See Figure 4.1. Alternatively the Housing and Urban Development contact information may be replaced by HUD regional information (Area Office stamp).]*

(b) The Assistant Secretary for Equal Opportunity may grant a waiver permitting the substitution of a poster prescribed by a Federal financial regulatory agency for the fair housing poster described in paragraph (a) of this section. While such waiver remains in effect, compliance with the posting requirements of such regulatory agency shall be deemed compliance with the posting requirements of this part. Such waiver shall not affect the applicability of all other provisions of this part.

24 CFR § 110.30 Effect of failure to display poster.

Any person who claims to have been injured by a discriminatory housing practice may file a complaint with the Secretary pursuant to part 105 of this chapter. A failure to display the fair housing poster as required by this part shall be deemed prima facie evidence of a discriminatory housing practice.

Creating Protected Class-Sensitive Advertising

Today, most complaints involving fair housing advertising are based on blatant violations of the Fair Housing Act, such as ads seeking "no children" or "adults only." However, with the increased scrutiny of real estate advertising by fair housing organizations, testers, and individual homeseekers, many real estate practitioners are concerned about being charged with housing bias based on the wording in their advertisements. Seemingly harmless words may trigger a complaint. The key to composing advertising that complies with the Fair Housing Act is to describe the property, not the seller, landlord, neighbors, or so-called appropriate buyers or renters.

Creating advertising that is sensitive to the protected classes under the Fair Housing Act is not as difficult as it may seem. Simply review the wording in the ad to see whether anyone might feel excluded by what is being said. Keep in mind that if a person wouldn't pick up the phone to respond to an ad because of exclusionary wording, the ad might generate a complaint. For example, the term Christian handyman in an ad for rental housing violated Wisconsin law by expressing illegal preferences on the basis of both sex and religion.

$835,000 Settlement Reached in Fair Housing Advertising Lawsuit—Spann v. Colonial Village *(Nos. 947075 and 947093)*

To settle a nearly ten-year-old lawsuit based on discriminatory advertising, a Virginia condominium and apartment complex and its corporate parent have agreed to pay the plaintiffs a record $835,000. The lawsuit was filed by Girardeau Spann, an African American law professor who lives in the District of Columbia, and two fair housing organizations.

The plaintiffs charged Colonial Village with the exclusive use of white human models in their ads. Before 1986, none of the human models used in newspaper advertising or brochures were black. However, the lawsuit never alleged denial of housing opportunity based on race. The defendants agreed to implement advertising policy that any human models used would reasonably represent both majority and minority groups in the metropolitan area.

Fair Housing Conciliation Agreement and MLS—67 Agreed-Upon Words

A conciliation agreement has been entered into between HUD, the Fair Housing Council of Oregon, and the Portland Metropolitan Area Boards and Associations of REALTORS® Multiple Listing Service, Inc. (RMLS™) regarding words in the RMLS ™ database that potentially violate the Fair Housing Act.

As part of the agreement, RMLS™ has agreed to conduct biweekly computerized searches of the "Remarks" section of all active listings to detect any of the words or phrases that the parties agreed RMLS ™ shall not use and to delete any such words. The list of agreed-upon words is below.

Please be cautious in how you use this list of words.

The list was the product of a negotiated settlement and not a ruling by a court or HUD, and HUD has not endorsed this list. Words not appearing on this list could be used to discriminate. Conversely, words appearing on the list will not always violate the law.

(Thanks to the Portland Metropolitan Area Boards and Associations of REALTORS® Multiple Listing Service for not including a confidentiality clause in the conciliation agreement so that others may learn from their experience.)

November 1995
Words that Will Not Be Used in the RMLS™

able bodied
adult community
adult living
adults only
African
agile
alcoholics, no
Asian
bachelor
blacks, no
board approval required
Catholic
Caucasian
Chicano
Chinese
children, no
colored
couple
couples only
crippled, no
deaf, no
drinkers, no
employed, must be
empty nesters (ethnic references)
handicapped, not for
healthy only
Hispanic
impaired, no
independent living
Indian
Irish
integrated
Jewish
landlord (description of)
Latino
married
mature couple
mature individual
mature person(s)
membership approval required
mentally handicapped, no
mentally ill, no
Mexican-American
Mormon Temple
Mosque (nationality)
Newlyweds
(# of) children
older person(s)
one child
one person
Oriental
physically fit
Polish
Puerto Rican
retarded, no
seasonal worker, no
shrine
singles only
single person
smoker(s), no
Soc. Sec. Ins. (SSI), no
tenant (description of)
unemployed, no
white
white only

Source: National Association of REALTORS®

Summary

Real estate professionals must have an in-depth understanding of the Fair Housing Act's prohibition of discriminatory advertising. All advertising, including newspaper and magazine ads, flyers, radio and television commercials, brochures, and even ads placed in phone books, must comply with fair housing laws. All forms of advertising in any media must not show a preference, limitation, or discrimination directed at the protected classes.

Any discriminatory statements made are illegal under the Fair Housing Act and HUD regulations. Real estate agents should carefully review all ads to ensure that no prohibited words or phrases are included. Remember, it is much safer to describe the property in terms of its physical characteristics than to target people who would be considered appropriate buyers or renters.

case study

The owners of Carolyn Apartments had placed an ad in a local telephone directory every year since the Fair Housing Amendments Act took effect in 1989. The act banned discrimination targeting families. The ad read "one bedroom, all adults." The words "All Adult" were painted on the front of the complex.

The Kentucky Fair Housing Council discovered the complex and tried to run tests for family status discrimination, but there were no vacancies at the Carolyn Apartments. Several drop-in tests were conducted and produced evidence that the apartments were not a seniors-only complex. No children were seen at the property during any of these tests.

The Fair Housing Council filed a lawsuit against the publisher of the phone book, claiming that it had run an ad in the yellow pages that discriminated against families with children.

1. Does the Fair Housing Act apply to publishers of telephone books?
2. What policies or procedures could the publisher implement that would assist it in not accepting ads that violate the Fair Housing Act?
3. What amount do you think the company agreed to pay to the Fair Housing Council to settle claims that it had run an ad discriminating against families?

Chapter 4 Review Questions

1. A housing provider who is exempt from the Fair Housing Act may place an ad indicating no children.
   a. True
   b. False

2. The *Hunter* opinion established that the Fair Housing Act
   a. does not apply to newspapers and other media.
   b. if applied to newspapers, would violate the First Amendment guarantee of freedom of the press.
   c. Both of these
   d. Neither of these

3. An advertisement containing which phrase would *LEAST* likely violate the Fair Housing Act?
   a. "Perfect for the sports enthusiast"
   b. "Bring the kids and the pets, too"
   c. "Accessible units available"
   d. "Executive home"

4. The case that stated that human models must reasonably represent majority and minority groups was *HUD v. RMSL*™.
   a. True
   b. False

5. The 1995 HUD memorandum on advertising prohibited which of the following terms?
   a. Bachelor apartment.
   b. Master bedroom.
   c. Both of these
   d. Neither of these

6. The key to composing advertising that complies with the act is to describe
   a. the seller.
   b. the landlord.
   c. appropriate buyers or renters.
   d. the property.

7. Newspapers who print the HUD Publisher's Notice can never be sued for violating the Fair Housing Act.
   a. True
   b. False

8. The use of the term *master bedroom* violates both the race and the sex discrimination provisions of the act.
   a. True
   b. False

9. Which statement regarding fair housing advertising is *TRUE*?
   a. Fair housing organizations are not concerned with fair housing advertising.
   b. Seemingly harmless words may trigger a complaint.
   c. Housing providers may selectively use the logotype and slogan.
   d. Advertising agencies cannot be sued for violating the act.

10. All of the following ads will violate the Fair Housing Act *EXCEPT*
    a. "No more than two children."
    b. "Perfect for empty nesters."
    c. "Exclusive home in private neighborhood."
    d. "Fisherperson's paradise."

chapter five

Fair Housing Enforcement

learning objectives

After completing this chapter, you will be able to

- discuss the HUD enforcement procedure,
- outline the enforcement role of the Justice Department,
- explain the process of filing a civil suit in federal district court, and
- explain how testers are utilized in the enforcement process.

Key Terms

aggrieved person	conciliation	punitive damages
complainant	conciliation agreement	respondent

The federal Fair Housing Act provides for three methods of enforcement of its substantive provisions. Although the original 1968 act did provide for the same methods of enforcement, the 1988 Fair Housing Amendments Act dramatically strengthened the enforcement mechanisms and remedies. The existing enforcement and remedies were virtually ineffective in combating housing discrimination. The 1988 Amendments Act sought to validate the promise of the 1968 act of providing a housing market free of discrimination.

The HUD enforcement procedure was transformed from a toothless system of conference, conciliation, and persuasion to one that provides for administrative and judicial hearings and a full range of serious sanctions and remedies. In private lawsuits, the statute of limitations was extended from 180 days to two years, and restrictions on punitive damages and attorney's fees were removed. The relief available in Justice Department suits was expanded to include monetary damages and civil penalties of up to $100,000.

The pace of fair housing litigation over the two decades following the passage of the Fair Housing Act in 1968 was modest, with the Supreme Court deciding only five cases during this 20-year period. The number of fair housing cases filed represented only a tiny fraction of the number of instances of illegal housing discrimination that were occurring every year in this country. Litigation in the field of fair housing law entered a period of rapid growth, primarily due to the passage of the 1988 Fair Housing Amendments Act. Fair housing complaints filed with HUD from 1988 to 1990 rose a dramatic 70 percent. Damage awards available to victims of housing discrimination continue to accelerate at a record-setting pace.

The U.S. Supreme Court issued a significant ruling in 1995 regarding group homes. In *City of Edmonds v. Oxford House*, the Court ruled that the occupancy standards exist to protect from overcrowding, not to preserve the "family character" of a neighborhood. This paved the way for establishment of group homes in neighborhoods throughout the country.

In 2003, the Supreme Court unanimously reversed the Ninth Circuit's *Holley* decision, which held that owners and officers of a corporation were vicariously liable under the Fair Housing Act and that a corporation and its officers may be liable to ensure the corporation's compliance with the Fair Housing Act, whether or not the officers directed or authorized the discriminatory conduct at issue. Salesperson Crank had allegedly prevented the buyers from purchasing a home for racially discriminatory reasons. The buyers eventually built their own home in the same town, and the home they initially intended to bid on eventually sold for a lower price. The buyers filed suit against *both* the brokerage and the broker personally. The Supreme Court, in reversing the Ninth Circuit, ruled that owners and officers of real estate agencies are not individually liable under the Fair Housing Act for the discriminatory acts of the firm's employees.

Enforcement Options

As a rule, the three enforcement options available to victims of housing discrimination operate separately and independently of one another, but the act does provide for a good deal of coordination among them. For example, a complainant whose claims are decided in a full hearing in a HUD proceeding would be barred from pursuing the matter further in a private lawsuit.

An **aggrieved person,** defined in Title VIII of the Civil Rights Act of 1988 as an individual who "claims to have been injured by a discriminatory housing practice" or "believes that such person will be injured by a discriminatory housing practice that is about to occur," has the following options available to redress the discrimination:

- Enforcement through HUD
- Enforcement through the Department of Justice
- Enforcement by means of a private lawsuit filed in federal district court

Standing to Sue

The Fair Housing Act does not define who may sue or who may be sued for violating the act. Obviously, persons who are the direct victims of housing discrimination are entitled to sue the responsible party. In addition, the Supreme Court has also recognized that a proper plaintiff includes virtually anyone who has been injured in any way by conduct that violates the law. Potential complainants include testers, fair housing organizations, residents who were denied the benefits of living in integrated communities, and real estate agents who lost commissions due to discriminatory conduct. The Supreme Court has made it clear that standing to sue was to be defined in terms as broad as those permitted by Article III of the Constitution.

U.S. Supreme Court Reviews Parties' Standing to Sue Under the Fair Housing Act—Havens Realty v. Coleman, 455 U.S. 363, 102 S. Ct. 1114 (1982)

The Court ruled that individuals and housing organizations have standing to sue under the Fair Housing Act. Coles, a black person, attempted to rent an apartment from Havens Realty and was falsely told that no apartments were available. Housing Opportunities Made Equal (HOME) sent testers to determine whether Havens was practicing racial steering. Coleman, a black tester, was told there were no vacancies, while Willis, a white tester, was told there were vacancies. Coles, HOME, Coleman, and Willis brought a class-action suit against Havens Realty.

The district court dismissed the claims, stating that the group lacked standing to sue. The court, however, heard Coles's claims and found that Havens had engaged in unlawful racial steering. Coleman, Willis, and HOME appealed to the Fourth Circuit, which ruled that Coleman and Willis had standing to sue in their capacities as testers and individuals. Havens appealed to the Supreme Court.

The Supreme Court ruled that HOME also had standing to sue as a fair housing organization and upheld the Fourth Circuit ruling regarding the testers' standing as well.

The Use of Testers

The U.S. Supreme Court has recognized that the use of testers is a necessary and essential means of enforcing this country's fair housing laws. The Fair Housing Act specifically provides that all persons have the right to receive true and accurate information regarding housing opportunities and to receive the same treatment that other persons receive without differences owing to race or other protected class factors. HUD regulations state that an "aggrieved person" includes "a fair housing organization as well as a tester or other person who seeks information regarding the availability of dwellings to determine whether discriminatory housing practices are occurring."

Testers have been described by the Supreme Court as "individuals who, without an intent to rent or purchase a home or apartment, pose as renters or purchasers for the purpose of collecting evidence of unlawful . . . practices." In fair housing cases based on racial discrimination, for example, white testers will attempt to determine if they will receive more favorable treatment by a potential defendant than a similarly situated black applicant. The evidence collected by the testers is then presented in court.

Testers may recover damages for humiliation, mental anguish, and emotional distress. The fact that testers might approach a housing provider without any intention of procuring housing and with the knowledge that they might experience discriminatory treatment is not considered relevant. Further, this does not impair credibility of testers as witnesses, nor does it negate their right to recover damages.

The Department of Justice, HUD, and fair housing organizations throughout the country are all conducting extensive testing. The Department of Justice has significantly expanded the Civil Rights Division's housing section, which will enable it to devote more time and resources to the testing initiative.

In 2009, the Fair Housing Council of Suburban Philadelphia published a report on voice profiling experienced by African American renters in the Philadelphia region. Testers with racially identifiable voices contacted landlords, apartment complex managers, and real estate agents in the region and objectively documented their experience to determine whether white testers were treated more favorably than African American testers. Results showed that in 54 percent of the tests, testers that sounded African American were treated less favorably than testers that sounded white. Compared with their white counterparts, African American testers were asked to pay higher security deposits, were offered fewer units, and were less likely to be told about discounts. In 8 percent of the tests, African American testers didn't receive return phone calls while white testers received return phone calls and information about available housing. The report concluded that despite enactment of the Fair Housing Act over 40 years ago, discrimination continues to limit housing choice in the Philadelphia region on the basis of race, disability, and familial status.

Disparate Treatment and Disparate Impact Theories of Discrimination

The disparate treatment theory of housing discrimination is easily understood because these cases typically involve intentional acts of discrimination directed at those protected by the law. Evidence of the discriminatory motive may be direct, as in a case with open hostility directed toward the minority or other protected group, or circumstantial, which is more often the case. Circumstantial evidence is evaluated based on the housing provider's business practices, with particular emphasis on statistical information regarding the past record of dealing with the protected class.

Aggrieved persons must establish that

- they are a member of a protected class,
- they were financially qualified to obtain the property,
- they were rejected by the defendant, and
- the housing opportunity remained open after the rejection.

The defendant must come forward with evidence of some legitimate nondiscriminatory reason for refusing to deal with the plaintiff.

The disparate impact theory of housing discrimination requires no evidence of discriminatory intent. Disparate impact cases generally involve policies or laws that cause disproportionate harm to members of a protected class. This form of discrimination can be subtle and even unconscious, but when the conduct at issue has a significant statistical effect of disfavoring those protected by law, the result is illegal discrimination. The defendant must present evidence of a business necessity to justify the challenged conduct. It is important to note that applying the criteria to everybody is not sufficient to demonstrate compliance with the Fair Housing Act. The disparate impact theory provides the means of holding housing providers liable for the results of their conduct.

Note:

The key to proving a disparate impact claim is statistical evidence showing that the defendant's practice has a greater impact on protected class members than on others. In *Betsey v. Turtle Creek Associates* (4th Cir. 1984), the court held that a landlord's policy of evicting families with children from one of its buildings had a "substantially greater adverse impact on minority tenants." Real estate professionals must be aware that seemingly innocent actions might constitute unlawful discrimination under the disparate impact theory.

The HUD Enforcement Procedure

Although the HUD enforcement procedure was dramatically changed by the 1988 Fair Housing Amendments Act, **conciliation** remains a primary tool for fair housing enforcement. It is important to note, however, that even though the 1968 act severely limited HUD's powers of enforcement, most people aggrieved by discriminatory housing practices have traditionally utilized the HUD administrative process for resolving housing discrimination complaints. Perhaps this is due to the advantages of enforcement through HUD. The greatest advantage may be that HUD offers free legal representation. In addition, the HUD-processed charge will likely be decided faster than a court suit. Finally, the decision maker in a HUD proceeding is an administrative law judge with a great deal of expertise in fair housing matters.

An aggrieved person may file a complaint with HUD within one year after an alleged discriminatory housing practice has occurred. **Complainants** may file in person, by mail, or by telephone. Each complaint must contain

- the name and address of the aggrieved person;
- the name and address of the respondent;
- a description and the address of the dwelling involved; and
- a concise statement of the facts, including pertinent dates, constituting the alleged discriminatory housing practice.

Note:

The 1988 Amendments Act requires that HUD refer complaints to state and local agencies whose fair housing laws have been certified as substantially equivalent to the federal statute. Within 30 days, the referral agency must commence proceedings. HUD will reactivate the case if the agency fails to do so. *See* the appendix.

The HUD Complaint Process

After receiving the complaint, HUD must advise the aggrieved party of the right to commence a civil action in federal district court no later than two years after the alleged discriminatory practice. (*See* Figure 5.1.) Within ten days, HUD must serve the **respondent** notice of the filing of the complaint. The notice, which contains a copy of the complaint, will also advise the respondent of the aggrieved person's right to commence a civil action. In addition, the respondent is informed of its procedural rights and obligations under the law. The respondent is entitled to file an answer within ten days after receipt of the notice.

Once the complaint is filed, HUD must investigate, attempt to resolve the complaint through conciliation, and either file a charge or dismiss the complaint. HUD may also refer the case to a "substantially equivalent" local or state agency, and in cases involving local zoning or other land-use ordinances, HUD will refer the matter to the Justice Department for further consideration. HUD may also refer a case to the attorney general if a situation requires prompt judicial action. For example, a temporary restraining order may be needed to prevent the defendant from selling or renting the dwelling to a third party.

Investigation and conciliation. The statute requires that HUD complete its investigation of the complaint within 100 days, unless it is impractical to do so. HUD must notify all parties if it is unable to meet the deadline.

From the time the complaint is filed, HUD must engage in conciliation efforts aimed at achieving a just resolution of the complaint. A **conciliation agreement** may include monetary damages and injunctive relief appropriate to the elimination of the discriminatory conduct. In addition, the conciliation agreement must contain provisions to vindicate public interest, including affirmative actions undertaken to remedy the effects of the discriminatory housing practices.

The written conciliation agreement is executed by the respondent and the complainant, and is subject to the approval of the secretary of HUD. A conciliation agreement precludes an aggrieved person from bringing a civil suit based on the same challenged conduct.

The issuance of a charge. Based on the facts of the investigation, HUD will find that reasonable cause exists that either a discriminatory housing practice has occurred or is about to occur, and it then will either issue a formal charge or dismiss the complaint after determining that no reasonable cause exists.

Within three business days after issuing a charge, HUD must file it with the Office of Administrative Law Judges and serve it on both the complainant and the respondent. Either party may, within 20 days after receipt of service of the charge, elect to have the charges decided by civil action rather than by a HUD administrative law judge (ALJ). If a judicial election is made, HUD will authorize the attorney general to commence an action within 30 days in an appropriate federal district court.

If the parties decide to have the matter settled in a HUD administrative proceeding, a hearing date must be set within three business days. The date of the hearing may not be later than 120 days following the issuance of the charge.

The decision. Within 60 days after the conclusion of the hearing, the ALJ must issue an initial decision based on findings of fact and conclusions of law. The initial decision will become final unless reviewed by the secretary of HUD within

Figure 5.1 | Fair Housing Complaint Process

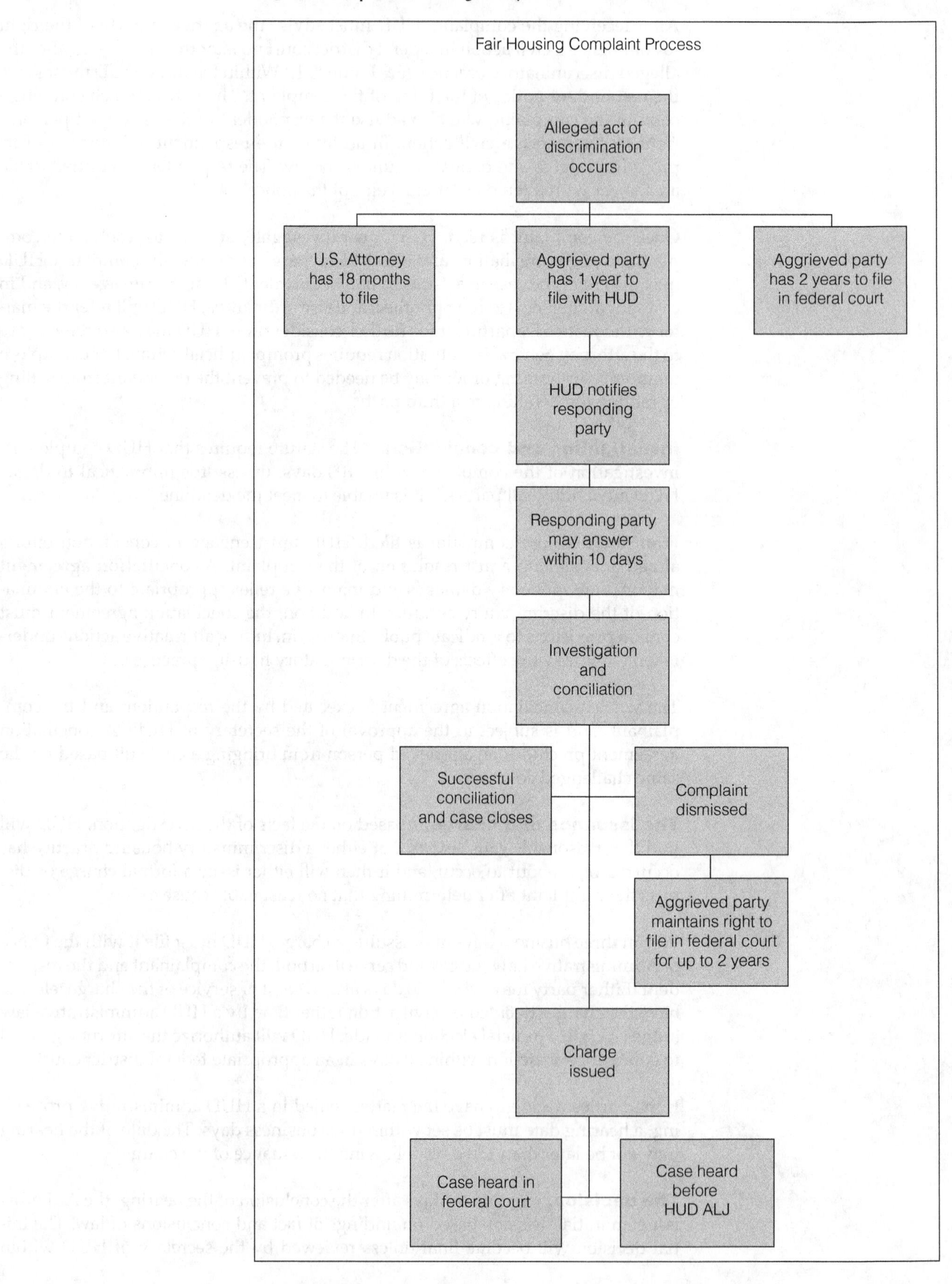

30 days. The secretary has the power to affirm or modify the ALJ's decision, to set aside the decision in whole or in part, or to remand the decision for further proceedings.

If the ALJ determines in the initial decision that the respondent has not engaged, or is not about to engage, in a discriminatory housing practice, the charge will be dismissed.

Relief available. If the ALJ determines that a discriminatory housing practice has occurred, the following relief may be ordered:

- Actual damages, including out-of-pocket expenses and monetary awards for embarrassment, humiliation, mental anguish, inconvenience, and other noneconomic awards
- Equitable relief, including access to the dwelling and the provision of services or facilities in connection with the dwelling
- Injunctive relief, preventing the defendant from discriminating in the future
- Civil penalties may be assessed against the respondent to vindicate public interest, in an amount not exceeding
  - $16,000 for a first offense,
  - $37,500 if there has been a prior offense within five years, and
  - $65,000 if there have been two or more offenses within seven years.

If a discriminatory housing practice has been found in a business that is subject to licensing and regulation by a government agency, HUD is required to notify the agency of the final decision and to recommend that appropriate disciplinary action be taken.

Judicial review. Any party adversely affected by a final decision may file a petition for review in an appropriate court of appeals within 30 days of the date of issuance of the final decision. The court has the power to affirm or modify the order, to set aside all or parts of the order, or to remand it for further proceedings. The court may also enforce the order to the extent that it has been affirmed or modified and order any further relief that it deems proper.

If no petition for review is filed within 45 days, the order will be conclusive in any further enforcement proceedings. HUD may petition a court of appeals for enforcement of the final order. If HUD does not seek enforcement of the final order within 60 days, any person entitled to relief may petition for enforcement.

HUD's Annual Report on Fair Housing, FY 2010

More than 10,000 fair housing discrimination complaints were filed with HUD and its Fair Housing Assistance Program partner agencies in fiscal year 2010. Discrimination based on a person's disability continued to be the largest single category of complaints: 48 percent of the complaints alleged disability discrimination, 34 percent alleged discrimination based on race and 15 percent alleged discrimination based on familial status. Complaints based on national origin accounted for 12 percent of the claims, while sex was the basis of 11 percent of the claims. Retaliation, religion, and color were the least common bases of complaints. Retaliation was cited as a basis in 7 percent, while religion was cited as a basis in 3 percent of the total claims, and just 2 percent of the claims were based on color.

The large number of complaints based on disability is due, in part, to the additional protections afforded persons with disabilities under the Fair Housing Act (i.e., reasonable accommodation, reasonable modification, and accessible design and construction).

The most common condition issue in complaints in 2010 was discriminatory terms, conditions, privileges, services, and facilities in the rental or sale of property (59 percent). Failure to make reasonable accommodations (25 percent) and refusal to rent (24 percent) were the second and third most common issues in complaints. Retaliation was cited as the issue in 15 percent of the complaints and discriminatory notices, statements, and advertising represented the discriminatory conduct in 9 percent of the complaints.

The complete report is available at *http://portal.hud.gov/hudportal/documents/huddoc?id=ANNUALREPORT2010.PDF*.

Enforcement by the Justice Department

The role of the Justice Department in enforcing the Fair Housing Act was greatly expanded by the 1988 Fair Housing Amendments Act. The Civil Rights Division's housing section was expanded under the Clinton administration to assist in litigating housing discrimination cases. The expansion enabled the Department of Justice (DOJ) and HUD to conduct joint investigations of financial institutions suspected of lending discrimination.

The Role of the Justice Department in Enforcement

The Justice Department is also authorized to prosecute cases involving the use of force or the threat of force to injure, intimidate, or interfere with people exercising their rights under the Fair Housing Act.

The Fair Housing Act authorizes DOJ to bring civil actions in three distinct situations. First, the attorney general may sue in a case involving a pattern or practice of housing discrimination or in a case that is considered to be of general public importance. Second, the attorney general is authorized to bring a civil action based on a referral from HUD in cases involving challenges to zoning and other land-use ordinances or if HUD believes that a respondent has breached a conciliation agreement. The Justice Department suit must be filed within 18 months of the HUD referral involving the challenged discriminatory land-use law. In the case of a breached conciliation agreement, the Justice Department must bring suit within 90 days of the referral. Third, the attorney general may file suit to enforce a subpoena issued in a HUD administrative proceeding.

The attorney general must also represent complainants in cases removed to federal district court after HUD has issued a formal charge. HUD may also request that the attorney general file a civil action in situations requiring prompt judicial action for appropriate temporary or preliminary relief, such as an order preventing the defendant from selling or renting the property to a third party.

Direct Court Actions

An aggrieved person may commence a civil action in an appropriate U.S. district court or state court without first filing a complaint with HUD not later than two years after the occurrence or termination of an alleged discriminatory housing practice or in the event of a breach of a conciliation agreement entered into in a HUD proceeding. The two-year period does not apply to actions arising from a breach of a conciliation agreement.

The 1988 Fair Housing Amendments Act made major changes in enforcement through private court action. The law extended the statute of limitations from 180 days to two years, removed the $1,000 cap on punitive damage awards, and made attorney's fee awards more readily available. It is important to note that the statute of limitations will be tolled during the time a complainant is involved in a HUD administrative proceeding.

Relief Available

The court may award actual damages resulting from the discriminatory conduct, such as expenses incurred in finding alternative housing. Most fair housing cases, however, do not involve large monetary losses. Most monetary awards have been to compensate the plaintiff for noneconomic injuries, such as embarrassment, humiliation, mental anguish, inconvenience, and similar intangible injuries. In determining the amount of such awards, the court will generally look at two factors:

- The egregiousness of the discriminatory conduct.
- The plaintiff's reaction to it. Some people are simply more deeply affected by being discriminated against.

Punitive damage awards are available in a civil action. Punitive damages are awarded to punish the defendant and to deter the defendant and others from engaging in similar conduct in the future. In 1983, the Supreme Court articulated in *Smith v. Wade* that punitive damage awards are appropriate, based not only on the defendant's malicious intent but also or whether the defendant's conduct demonstrated a "reckless or callous disregard of or indifference to" the plaintiff's rights. Types of conduct that satisfy the reckless indifference standard include the following:

- Racially discriminatory statements
- Differential treatment
- Covering up discriminatory housing practices
- Lies about availability
- Refusal to deal with protected classes
- Knowledge of illegality

Punitive damage awards have ranged from as little as $250 to as much as $2 million.

The court may order injunctive relief, that is, relief that would prevent the defendant from violating the Fair Housing Act in the future.

Equitable relief may be granted under the Fair Housing Act for the purpose of removing any lingering effects of past discrimination.

The court may also grant any other relief that the court deems appropriate, including any permanent or temporary injunction, temporary restraining order, or other order enjoining the defendant from engaging in the discriminatory housing practice. The Fair Housing Act states, however, that an order may not "affect any contract, sale, encumbrance, or lease consummated before the granting of such relief and involving a bona fide purchaser, encumbrancer, or tenant, without actual notice of the filing of a complaint with the Secretary or civil action under this title." This obviously is for the protection of innocent buyers or renters and would prevent them from losing their homes in the absence of a court order. In other words, the simple filing of a claim under the Fair Housing Act would not in itself be sufficient to prevent a bona fide purchaser or renter from obtaining the housing.

Summary

It is important that real estate agents understand the enforcement mechanisms of the Fair Housing Act. The act can be violated even when there is no intention to do so. Real estate agents should examine their business practices to determine whether any would cause disproportionate harm to members of a protected class. It must be emphasized again that agents must be aware of additional protected groups, either locally or at the state level. Some states, like Virginia, have more severe fines under their state fair housing law.

case study

Albert Lepieux owned a mobile home park that he operated as an all-adult complex. When the 1988 Amendments Act took effect, he made no effort to qualify his property as housing for older persons, but he continued his policy of excluding children, even though families with kids were now a protected class. He did consider the putting green and the bar on site to represent "significant services and facilities" for adults.

Jack and Julie Good lived at Lepieux's mobile home park and in the summer of 1989 tried to sell their mobile home. The only offers came from families with children, and Lepieux adamantly refused to allow the sale. Tension mounted and Lepieux began opening the Goods' mail and refused to do any repairs on their property.

The Goods filed a complaint with HUD alleging discrimination based on familial status. HUD determined after investigating the complaint that an act of discrimination likely occurred and issued a charge. At this point, Lepieux removed the case from HUD and proceeded with trial in federal district court. The court awarded the Goods $150,000, which was upheld on appeal.

1. Why would Lepieux want to remove the case from HUD?
2. Do you think the damage award would have been as great if the case had been decided by HUD?

Chapter 5 Review Questions

1. An aggrieved person must first file a complaint with HUD before filing in federal district court.
   a. True
   b. False

2. Plaintiffs who have standing to file a discrimination lawsuit under the Fair Housing Act include
   a. testers.
   b. current residents of a cooperative association.
   c. Both of these
   d. Neither of these

3. The advantages of filing a direct court action include
   a. free legal representation.
   b. a speedier resolution of the complaint.
   c. a decision maker with a great deal of expertise in fair housing matters.
   d. the availability of punitive damages.

4. Aggrieved persons may file a complaint with HUD for
   a. up to 180 days.
   b. up to one year.
   c. up to two years.
   d. an unlimited period.

5. HUD must complete its investigation of a fair housing complaint within
   a. 180 days.
   b. 90 days.
   c. 120 days.
   d. 100 days.

6. Which statement is *TRUE* regarding fair housing enforcement?
   a. An aggrieved person does not include testers.
   b. The disparate impact theory requires no evidence of discriminatory intent.
   c. Conciliation is no longer a primary tool for fair housing enforcement.
   d. HUD must complete its investigation within 180 days.

7. The disparate treatment theory provides the means of holding housing providers liable for the results of their conduct.
   a. True
   b. False

8. The maximum civil penalty that can be assessed by a HUD administrative law judge is
   a. $16,000.
   b. $37,500.
   c. $65,000.
   d. $75,000.

9. The maximum civil penalty available in a lawsuit by the Justice Department is
   a. $25,000.
   b. $50,000.
   c. $75,000.
   d. $100,000.

10. The statute of limitations for a fair housing discrimination lawsuit in federal district court is
    a. 180 days.
    b. one year.
    c. two years.
    d. no existing limitation.

chapter six

Cultural Diversity and Fair Housing

learning objectives

After completing this chapter, you will be able to

- define diversity;
- explain bias, stereotype, and prejudice;
- point out practices that constitute steering; and
- respond to questions regarding neighborhood ethnicity.

Key Terms

bias	diversity	stereotype
culture	steering	

"I am not an Athenian or a Greek, but a citizen of the world." —Socrates

Data from the 2010 U.S. census confirmed that America is rapidly becoming a truly multicultural society. The U.S. Census Bureau reports minorities now constitute just over one-third of the nation's population. This group increased from 86.9 million to 111.9 million between 2000 and 2010, representing a growth of 29 percent over the decade. Minority groups are growing much faster as a percentage of the population than non-Hispanic whites. Nearly 9 million Americans identify themselves as multiracial, which is about 3 percent of the total population.

The University of Georgia's Selig Center for Economic Growth reports that between 1990 and 1991 alone, minority consumerism grew 54 percent. Diversity increasingly shapes housing markets. Over this decade, minorities are expected to contribute fully two-thirds—and immigrants alone more than one-quarter—to the expected growth in households.

The 21st century real estate professional must understand and respect cultural diversity to deal effectively with persons from different cultures. The National Association of REALTORS® has indicated that in recent years, the United States has received the largest number of immigrants since the 1930s, an estimated 1 million new immigrants each year, and after six years, two-thirds of immigrants enter the homebuying market. This represents a great opportunity for salespersons to expand their clientele base.

Cultural Diversity Defined

Diversity is a word that relates to the uniqueness of each individual. Diversity also describes the variety that exists with respect to race, ethnicity, religion, gender, age, familial and marital status, sexual orientation, and physical or mental capabilities. Fair housing laws also protect these groups.

Diversity can also describe differences in personality traits, such as being an extrovert or an introvert, or one's job or profession and educational level.

Culture is defined as values, beliefs, behaviors, language, thought processes, and customs shared by a group of people. Culture teaches us how to function within our own group and defines how we view the world—in other words, what is proper to feel, think, say, and do. When people from one culture use their values and standards to attempt to understand another culture, the result usually is a clash of cultural orientations.

There is a strong tendency to assume that others are similar to us. Sigmund Freud called this projection. This assumption may work well when dealing with people from the same or similar cultures, but it is usually not successful when a different culture is involved. Therefore, to succeed in the multicultural marketplace, the real estate professional must value diversity and learn as much as possible about the client's culture. No culture is universal, and no practice is common to all.

The Cycle: Bias, Stereotype, Prejudice

Bias can be defined as a preference or preconceived opinion or point of view that does not allow impartiality in interpretation. We were all raised with biases, and they are rooted in generalizations we formed as we grew up.

When these generalizations are applied to all members of a particular group, they become **stereotypes.** Often these stereotypes are seen as weaknesses and will result in prejudice.

It is important that salespersons not make assumptions or stereotype a consumer based on cultural differences. Stereotyping can easily lead to misunderstandings, and often assumptions prove to be wrong. It is important not to assume that people from a particular culture will desire to live in an area occupied by people from the same culture. Assuming such a preference and identifying neighborhoods based on this could result in illegal steering. The right to live in the neighborhood of one's choosing is guaranteed in this country.

One solution might be to have the consumer fill out a needs-and-wants questionnaire to determine exactly what the consumer wants, while at the same time giving the consumer the opportunity to set any limits that are deemed important. For example, an Asian couple might want the front door to face a certain direction because of a religious belief. Others may express a preference not to have certain numbers present in an address, based on Chinese numerology, a system where some numbers are considered lucky and others are not, based on how they sound.

An Embarrassing Moment . . .

Eleanor Roosevelt once was seated at an official luncheon next to a Chinese official she had never met. Although he was well dressed and obviously important, he never spoke. The first lady assumed that his English must be poor, so in an attempt at conversation she asked, "Likee soupee?" He smiled and nodded graciously. Minutes later, he arose and proceeded to deliver the keynote address in perfect English. Upon returning to his seat, Mr. Koo, China's ambassador to the United States and a graduate of Harvard Law School, asked a red-faced Eleanor Roosevelt, "Likee speechee?" This story illustrates how often assumptions can be proven wrong and how embarrassing it can be when it happens!

Building Rapport with People from Other Cultures

Culture can play a significant role in the homebuying process. To establish the necessary rapport to successfully complete a real estate transaction, it is imperative that the salesperson understand the cultural differences that exist and what impact they will have on the transaction.

Establishing rapport is easiest between individuals or groups who share cultural attitudes. It is usually only possible to establish rapport with individuals who feel accepted.

Often it is easier to establish rapport than it is to keep it. It is okay to ask questions and, as previously mentioned, to learn as much as possible about a particular culture or religion. Recognizing the issues that are important to multicultural clients will enable the salesperson to successfully work with persons from different cultures.

Even a small misstep can threaten or even destroy a business relationship with a consumer. For example, many Asian businesspeople have a high reverence for business cards. A real estate agent who writes on the card, or puts the card in a back pocket and sits on it, probably has irreparably insulted the individual! Exchanging gifts in a business setting is highly cultural, but exercise caution in determining what is fitting. For instance, in Mexico and Brazil, purple flowers are associated with death.

Meeting and Greeting

Both men and women in the United States normally greet one another with a smile, a handshake, and possibly a hug. In other cultures, bowing is the traditional greeting, and kissing is the common way to greet in still other cultures. Even in cultures where bowing is traditional, variation exists in how people bow. For instance, in

Japan the depth of the bow, as well as the number of bows, is associated with respect. Thais bow with their hands together about chest-high as though they are praying.

Eye contact is treated differently in many cultures. In the United States, steady eye contact is the norm and indicates honesty and a sincere interest in the other party. But in some countries, avoiding eye contact is a sign of respect for the speaker. These differences in attitudes toward eye contact can be misunderstood and cause problems in maintaining rapport.

Real estate agents should also be aware that the personal space we are used to here often varies from culture to culture. In the United States, most are comfortable in the two-foot to four-foot range. In many cultures, it is considered rude to maintain more than a six-inch space when conducting business. An agent who backpedals when a client speaks right into his face will probably insult the person and lose rapport.

Decision Making

Decision making and negotiating strategies are greatly influenced by culture. Different cultures arrive at truth in different ways. These ways can be categorized as faith, fact, and feeling.

There are three generally recognized styles of decision making: individual, collaborative, and consensus. The individual style involves a single decision maker. In many cultures, the male is expected to dominate. Two or more individuals of equal or unequal influence contribute to the decision-making process in the collaborative style, and no decision is made using the consensus style until all parties affected by the decision can agree. Many cultures expect each individual to consider, "What is best for my family?"

Persons raised in a theocratic culture will negotiate and make decisions in a manner that will not conflict with their religious dogma.

The salesperson successful at building rapport with the largest group of multicultural clients is the salesperson who accepts and values all styles of decision making and understands the degree of influence family and religion play in the decision-making process.

Contracts and Negotiating

People from different cultures can have very different ideas about writing contracts and negotiating. In the United States, every detail from purchase price to closing date to inspections is written into the contract. In other countries, such as Mexico, China, and Japan, much more is implied and not actually spelled out in the contract. Some cultures feel that putting everything in writing implies mistrust.

The pace of negotiations is highly cultural. Here, we want to get down to business and propel the transaction to fruition. In some cultures, negotiating is a socialization process, like the American cocktail party. The Chinese are known for taking their time and trying to wear down the other side in order to get the best price. They also use this tactic to kill the transaction without losing face.

Each culture has its own unique negotiating style, and in many cultures, it is considered good business form to continue negotiating even after the final contracts have been signed. People from these "negotiating" countries take great pride in the bargaining skills that they have acquired over their lifetimes. They must believe that they got a "good deal" or they likely will not go through with it.

Establishing trust is a prerequisite to successful negotiations, but different cultural groups establish trust in different ways. Understanding how multicultural clients negotiate will help ensure a successful real estate transaction.

Time Awareness

Attitude toward time is highly cultural, with some cultures valuing it highly while others give it little to no value. In America we often say that "time is money" and place great value on promptness and getting down to business. People from certain cultures, like Germany and Australia, value promptness even more than Americans, and being a minute late is considered rude. On the other hand, being 15 to 30 minutes late is quite acceptable in countries like Japan. The Japanese may be late, but they will expect you to be on time because waiting for them is a sign of respect.

It is important that members of the real estate profession ascertain any differences in attitudes toward time to ensure success when working with different cultural groups.

The Role That Beliefs Play in the Real Estate Transaction

Cultural beliefs and practices may play a key role in the purchase of a home, and it is wise to find out early what beliefs clients may have, regardless of their culture, that may affect their purchase of real estate. By having all clients fill out a needs-and-wants questionnaire, the real estate agent can determine exactly what the client's preferences are regarding floor plans, colors, and how many bedrooms and bathrooms, as well as any special features they may require.

Some cultures have no beliefs that might affect the homebuying process, while others hold deeply rooted beliefs that highly influence their decision to purchase a particular property. For instance, Middle Easterners, Pakistanis, and Haitians tend to prefer one-story homes. Some Asian groups have religious beliefs that dictate the direction the front door faces.

Feng Shui

Feng shui is an ancient Chinese philosophy. The name literally means "wind and water." The goal of feng shui is to improve the flow of energy, or chi, in a person's environment, thus improving the flow of energy in the person. This belief system centers around the role of natural harmony of the five elements found in nature—wood, fire, earth, metal, and water. The beliefs associated with feng shui are too extensive for this book, but the real estate professional who works with a client who adheres to this belief system must have a basic knowledge of it to understand how those beliefs will affect the real estate transaction.

Feng shui teaches that bad luck travels in straight lines that create "secret arrows," while good luck travels along curved paths. For those who believe in feng shui strongly, curved or spiral staircases are preferred. Stairways facing the front door are considered bad because bad luck can enter and good luck can leave. The stove and the sink must not stand opposite each other because fire and water do not mix.

Many followers of feng shui will not want a house on a T-intersection or a home situated on a cul-de-sac. People living in these settings can experience health, financial, or relationship problems. Bad luck can travel down a street creating secret arrows and can go straight into the home.

Colors have particular significance in feng shui. For instance, red denotes fire and can bring fame and fortune. Wealth is represented by the colors green, red, and purple. Family is connected to the color green, and children to the color white. Yellow represents earth, while black is associated with one's career. Red, pink, and white all have special meaning for marital happiness.

Numerology

Belief in numerology can also affect the homebuying decisions of multicultural clients. In many Asian countries, the number 8 is considered lucky and the number 4, unlucky. In Chinese dialects, these numbers are homophones. The word for the number 8 sounds like the word for *rich* or *luck*, while the word for the number *4* sounds very close to the word for *death*. Koreans' lucky numbers are *3* and *7*, and again the number *4* is considered unlucky because of the same association with death.

In America, many are superstitious about the number 13 and would not want to be treated on the 13th floor of a hospital. For that matter, some buildings do not even have a 13th floor, and the elevator goes from the 12th floor to the 14th floor!

Numerology affects the purchase of real estate in several ways. First, numbers in the address are very important. For example, a house with the address of 444 would not likely be selected by an Asian. On the other hand, numbers that are considered good luck will influence a decision to buy, and certain number combinations will be used in the offer price to enhance health, wealth, and prosperity.

People from certain cultures hold strongly to various beliefs. It is essential that real estate agents understand how these beliefs will influence the real estate transaction.

Death in the Home

Having a death occur in a home can be a significant issue for many people, especially Asian homebuyers. Some Asians, as well as people from other cultures, will not want to live in a home connected with a death. They feel that they might inherit the bad luck from the previous owner of the property.

The Japanese traditionally avoid homes associated with murder, suicide, homicide, and other catastrophic events, because they do not wish to take advantage of others' misfortunes. Many Americans will also avoid homes with a negative history. The buyer of O. J. Simpson's property in California tore the house down and built a new one in its place to get rid of the negative history.

Most states have laws that property stigmas such as murder and other felony crimes do not need to be disclosed. Even if state law dictates that certain stigmas do not need to be disclosed, disclosure may still be the best way to avoid liability. In the late 1980s, an Asian couple purchased a home in California where the seller's son-in-law had hung himself in the basement. The neighbors disclosed this to the purchasers after they had moved in. The purchasers sued the seller and the listing agent for not disclosing this information. Because California has a stigmatized property law that states that the death did not need to be disclosed, the defendants prevailed in the lawsuit. Disclosing this information on a voluntary basis, however, would have prevented the lawsuit because the couple would have purchased a different property.

Steering

Steering is the practice of channeling minority homeseekers to designated areas and not permitting them access to all available housing. Steering is not a refusal to sell or rent, but rather a practice that makes certain housing unavailable. The Supreme Court has defined racial steering as "directing prospective home buyers interested in equivalent properties to different areas according to their race." Courts have held that steering violates the Fair Housing Act's "otherwise make unavailable or deny" provision.

Steering can take various forms. First, a housing provider may steer within its own units by keeping certain dwellings off limits to certain people. Second, individuals who feel they were not shown property in certain areas may bring a claim against a real estate professional. Third, neighborhood residents who, though not steered themselves, claim that the steering actions of others have destroyed the racial balance of their neighborhood or community may bring lawsuits.

Although the early court cases involving steering were based on allegations of racial discrimination, case law is currently developing with respect to handicap and familial status discrimination.

HUD Regulations

HUD regulations strongly endorse the view that the Fair Housing Act condemns steering. According to HUD's general definition of steering, it is unlawful on the basis of race or any other prohibited ground

to restrict or to attempt to restrict the choices of a person by word or conduct in connection with seeking, negotiating for, buying, or renting a dwelling so as to perpetuate, or tend to perpetuate, segregated housing patterns, or to discourage or obstruct choices in a community, neighborhood, or development.

The four specific examples of prohibited actions under this general definition of illegal steering are as follows:

- Engaging in any conduct related to the provision of housing or of services or facilities that otherwise makes unavailable or denies dwellings to protected persons
- Discouraging any person from inspecting, purchasing, or renting a dwelling on account of race, color, religion, sex, handicap, familial status, or national origin by exaggerating drawbacks, and failing to inform any person of desirable features of a dwelling or neighborhood
- Communicating to any persons that they would not be compatible with existing residents of a community because of their protected class status
- Assigning any person to a particular section of a community, neighborhood, or dwelling, or to a particular floor of a building, because or race, color, reli-

gion, sex, handicap, familial status, or national origin, a practice also known as steering

Responding to Questions Regarding Neighborhood Ethnicity

On arriving in this country, it is natural for immigrants to want to associate with people from their own ethnic group. Therefore, real estate professionals may be asked to identify neighborhoods based on ethnic considerations. For that matter, buyer's agents might be asked the same question by buyers wishing to limit the housing search based on race or other protected classes. Whether identifying neighborhoods based on race or other protected class factors, even at the request of the client, violates fair housing law prohibitions against steering has been the subject of considerable debate.

What about the situation where a client states a housing preference based on race or other protected class factors? The case law is mixed on the issue. In *Zuch v. Hussey,* one of the earliest and most influential opinions on steering, the court determined that a salesperson's efforts to influence a customer's housing choice on racial grounds would violate the Fair Housing Act, regardless of whether those efforts were undertaken on the salesperson's initiative or in response to the buyer's initiative. In *Zuch,* the defendant's behavior was so clearly an effort to influence choice on racial grounds that the court did not examine the issue of whether a salesperson is allowed to make any mention of the racial makeup of neighborhoods in dealing with customers (*Zuch v. Hussey,* 394 F. Supp. 1029, 1047 [E.D. Mich. 1975]).

In *Village of Bellwood v. Dwividi,* a 1990 Seventh Circuit case, the court held that the Fair Housing Act does not bar real estate brokers from showing black customers homes in integrated and predominantly black neighborhoods and white customers homes in predominantly white areas if the reason for such differential treatment is simply an effort to cater to the customer's own racial preferences. According to Robert Schemm, author of *Housing Discrimination Law & Litigation,* "*Dwividi* provides a strong endorsement for an agent's right to respond to customer-initiated racial inquiries." A key issue would be who initiates the discussion of race. In his decision, the judge made the distinction between brokers who deliberately try to alter customer's preferences in favor of racial segregation and brokers who honestly try to serve their customers (*Village of Bellwood v. Dwividi,* 895 F.2d 1521, 1529-34 [7th Cir. 1990]).

In 1996, Elizabeth Julian, assistant secretary for fair housing at HUD, issued two letters to the legal counsel of the buyer's agent, located in Germantown, Tennessee, attempting to answer specific questions regarding accommodating a buyer's discriminatory preferences. The resulting HUD opinion created widespread controversy, so much so that on December 3, 1996, HUD rescinded the opinion that allowed buyer's agents to show homes in specific neighborhoods if the buyer made the request based on race or other protected class factors. Julian stated, "She sent the wrong message." The position had been strongly opposed by fair housing organizations and the National Association of REALTORS®. The NAR staff felt that the original opinion might be seen as steering.

The National Association of REALTORS®, in a training manual, recommends "that a buyer's agent include language in his or her buyer's representation agreement indicating a commitment to equal housing opportunity and a statement that the agent has no duty to disclose information regarding race or other protected classes."

So, what then is the solution regarding situations where clients state a housing preference based on race or other protected class factors? One possibility would be to direct buyers to cultural clubs and organizations that might have access to statistical information regarding racial or ethnic makeup of various neighborhoods. Obtaining the information from sources such as these would not violate the Fair Housing Act. Buyers could then request that a real estate agent show homes in specific neighborhoods that they have identified that meet their housing needs. A real estate agent who refuses to show buyers homes in these areas risks violating the act by not making all housing available.

Court Asked to Determine If Agent Had Fiduciary Duty to Identify Ethnic Makeup of Neighborhood—Hannah v. Sibcy Cline Realtors® *(Ohio Ct. App. 2001)*

The court was asked to determine whether a real estate agent or a broker has the fiduciary duty to (1) inform a client whether a neighborhood or community is ethnically diverse or (2) direct the client to sources to provide ethnic diversity information. The Hannahs wanted a home in an ethnically diverse neighborhood in an excellent school district. They specifically did not want their son to be the only African American boy in his class. The agent informed them she could not give them that information, but she did send them school guidebooks. The Hannahs purchased a home in a neighborhood after the principal of the school indicated that the school was ethnically diverse. They then sued the real estate agent when their child turned out to be the only African-American boy in his third-grade class.

The trial court ruled that the Hannahs had not demonstrated that a real estate professional had a duty to inform the client whether a neighborhood was ethnically diverse or to direct the client to resources concerning this information. The appeals court upheld the decision and further stated that to avoid claims of unlawful steering in violation of the Fair Housing Act, it would not be in the best interests of an agent or broker to do so. The court concluded that imposing such a duty on real estate agents or brokers to give information about the ethnic makeup of a neighborhood would prove detrimental to the goal of fair housing.

Niche Marketing

The Fair Housing Act does not prohibit a person from marketing real estate services to any particular culture or group—for example, advertising in newspapers, phone books, and various other media that target the interests of diverse cultures would be appropriate.

Certain groups would not be covered by the federal Fair Housing Act. For example, one's profession would not be a protected class. A real estate licensee could target people such as doctors or lawyers without running afoul of the act.

Knowing Your Audience

Real estate agents must have a basic understanding of a particular culture before attempting to market their real estate services to them. Language pitfalls abound. General Motors found this out the hard way when it attempted to market the Chevy Nova in Mexico and South America. The sales were dismal and millions of dollars wasted because no one bothered to realize that Nova sounded like the Spanish phrase *no va*, which means "it doesn't go." Also, multicultural clients must be marketed to in the way they want to be reached, and this varies from culture to culture. What works for some cultures can have disastrous results in others. For example, using red ink or red paper to advertise in Chinese is good because in that culture, red represents good luck and prosperity. However, red is the Koreans' color of death and would be highly inappropriate.

An estimated 80 percent of Hispanics listen to Spanish-speaking radio stations, and 75 percent of Hispanics watch Spanish-speaking television stations. Real estate professionals could advertise their real estate services in the Spanish language to reach a large segment of this group.

Although some cultural groups, such as Asians, prefer to obtain information from reading newspapers, many multicultural clients do not customarily find real estate agents through newspaper ads or the yellow pages. They simply rely on references provided by trusted family and friends. Having a satisfied diverse clientele base can contribute enormously to the future success of the real estate professional.

What the Multicultural Client Looks for in an Agent

Multicultural clients are primarily interested in the quality of the person they choose to represent them. Personal characteristics such as sincerity, honesty, integrity, and patience are more important than credentials, degrees, and designations. Meaning what you say, keeping promises, responding honestly to questions, and doing what you say you are going to do defines the person that the multicultural client is looking for as an agent.

It is not typical that people from a particular culture will automatically seek out a real estate professional from the same culture. That's a good thing because the sales force in the United States is overwhelmingly Caucasian. Real estate professionals who do not recognize the importance of learning to work with diverse cultures are really missing the boat. After all, even Americans have beliefs that other cultures find difficult to understand.

Summary

In today's real estate market, there is tremendous opportunity to help multicultural people reach their dream of buying property in America. Brokers and salespersons must become aware of the different needs of people from other cultures if they wish to successfully complete the real estate transaction. By learning about deeply ingrained cultural tendencies and beliefs, real estate professionals will be able to better develop a basic understanding about the culture. Success in relationships with people from different cultures means learning the specialized ways of doing business with them. Real estate agents must also be aware of steering practices, which are illegal under the Fair Housing Act, and know how to properly respond when a client asks to limit the housing search based on race or other protected class status.

Additional Resources

Lee, Michael D. 1999. *Opening Doors: Selling to Multicultural Clients.* Winchester, Va.: Oakhill Press.

Streater, Carmel. 1999. *Diversity and Doing Business.* Chicago: Real Estate Education Company.

Morrison, Terri, Wayne A. Conaway, and George Borden. 1994. *Kiss, Bow, or Shake Hands.* Holbrook, Mass.: Adams Media Corporation.

case study

An Asian couple and their two children contacted Dylan Realty to look for a new home to purchase. When they visited the office for the first time, they were referred to the only Asian real estate agent in the company. They did not make a special request to work with an agent of a similar ethnic heritage.

Agent Sally Wong did not ask her new clients, the Lees, to fill out a needs-and-wants questionnaire and only asked them a few basic questions regarding size, price, and number of bedrooms and bathrooms they were looking for. She then selected a few neighborhoods known to her to have a high Asian population. They eventually purchased a home, but they had a nagging feeling that they weren't shown all the available housing and weren't offered a variety of choices with respect to neighborhoods.

1. Did Dylan Realty violate the Fair Housing Act by referring the Lee family to the only Asian agent? If yes, explain why.
2. Did Wong illegally steer her clients to certain neighborhoods? If your answer is yes, explain how.
3. If the Lee family directed Wong to show them homes only in areas that were predominately Asian, how should she have responded to this request?

Chapter 6 Review Questions

1. Valuing diversity is *NOT* important in working with multicultural clients.
   a. True
   b. False

2. Which statement is *TRUE* regarding eye contact?
   a. Avoiding eye contact is a sign of disrespect in all cultures.
   b. In the United States, maintaining steady eye contact indicates sincerity and interest.
   c. Both of these.
   d. Neither of these.

3. Which statement is *FALSE?*
   a. The Japanese may be late to an appointment but expect you to be on time.
   b. In America, we say, "Time is money."
   c. People from Germany and Australia are usually late for appointments.
   d. Attitude toward time is highly cultural.

4. People from "negotiating" countries cease negotiations after the purchase agreement is signed.
   a. True
   b. False

5. Colors in feng shui are important. Which statement is *TRUE?*
   a. Red denotes fire and can bring fame and fortune.
   b. The color green means money in feng shui.
   c. Both of these.
   d. Neither of these.

6. The court ruling that stated that real estate agents may never influence a customer's housing choice on racial grounds, even in response to a buyer's initiative, was
   a. *Village of Bellwood v. Dwividi.*
   b. *Zuch v. Hussey.*
   c. *Hannah v. Sibcy Cline* REALTORS®.
   d. none of these.

7. Having a death occur in a property is *ALWAYS* a significant issue for people.
   a. True
   b. False

8. The Fair Housing Act permits assigning people of the same culture to a particular section of a building.
   a. True
   b. False

9. Which statement regarding *Hannah v. Sibcy Cline* REALTORS® is *TRUE*?
   a. The court ruled that real estate agents have a fiduciary duty to inform a client of the ethnic diversity of a neighborhood.
   b. The agent is required to direct clients to sources where they can obtain information regarding the ethnic makeup of an area.
   c. Both of these.
   d. Neither of these.

10. The Fair Housing Act prohibits persons from marketing their real estate services to any particular culture or group.
    a. True
    b. False

chapter seven

Fair Housing Case Studies

learning objectives

After completing this chapter, you will be able to

- illustrate how HUD and the courts are continuing to develop and implement fair housing law,
- recognize discriminatory housing practices through case study analysis,
- describe the nature of damage awards from both HUD and the courts, and
- determine what relief you would order if you were the judge.

The following case studies are all based on actual HUD cases involving housing discrimination. The cases involve different protected groups and various discriminatory housing practices.

■ *HUD v. Blackwell*, Stone Mountain, Georgia, No. HUDALJ 048905201

Gordon Blackwell, sole owner of the property located at 4010 Indian Lakes Circle in Stone Mountain, Georgia, has been a licensed real estate broker for more than 20 years. Blackwell entered into a 90-day exclusive listing with Coldwell Banker agent Don Wainwright at $104,000, which was lowered to $98,000 after approximately 45 days. Blackwell told Wainwright, "Bring me an offer for $92,000 and I'll take it." On the profile sheet, it was noted that "super motivated seller wants offer" and would consider paying closing costs and discount points.

Blackwell subsequently entered into a purchase agreement with the Herrons, a black couple with two children, at a purchase price of $92,000, with the seller paying closing costs and discount points. However, upon discovering that the buyers were black, the seller changed the terms of the contract to require that the buyer pay closing costs. He refused to discuss the matter with Wainwright, changed the locks on the house, removed the lockbox, and refused to go to the scheduled closing.

Blackwell executed a lease with the Coopers, a white couple from Dallas, who had no prior knowledge of the pending transaction with the Herrons. Three days before the Coopers moved into the home, on July 24, 1989, the Herrons filed a complaint with HUD, alleging racial discrimination. A federal district court issued a temporary restraining order prohibiting Blackwell from renting or selling the property. Despite continual reassurances from Blackwell that the house was theirs, the Coopers retained an attorney and, fearing for their safety, changed the locks. Wainwright continued to make efforts to "close" the transaction. Blackwell refused to cooperate in any way, and was eventually held in contempt of court for failing to obey the preliminary injunction.

The Coopers moved out of the Indian Lakes Circle property and joined in the lawsuit against Blackwell.

ORDER

INJUNCTIVE RELIEF: ____________________

____

____

____

COMPENSATORY RELIEF: ____________________

____

____

CIVIL PENALTIES: ____________________

You Be the Judge

HUD v. Blackwell

1. What discriminatory housing practice would you cite in this case study?

2. Could Wainwright join in the lawsuit against Blackwell?

3. How was Blackwell protected by the decision to have the case determined by an HUD administrative law judge?

4. Were the Coopers victims of housing discrimination?

5. If you were the HUD administrative law judge, what relief would you order?

■ *HUD v. Dibari*, Jamaica Plain, Massachusetts, No. HUDALJ 019005111

Sara Kirschenbaum was six months pregnant when she and her husband, Bud Bedell, attempted to rent apartment #5, a four-room unit in a building located at 21 Woodman Street, Jamaica Plain, Massachusetts. The building owners, John and Grace Dibari, were immigrants to this country for whom English was a second language. Mr. Dibari, who was 75 years old, was ill with dizzy spells, "high sugar," and diabetes. Mr. Dibari stayed home caring for his wife, who was extremely ill and homebound. Other than Social Security, rent from their apartments was their only income. Most of their nine apartments remained unrented because the Dibaris didn't have the money to clean and repair them.

John Dibari instructed his listing agent not to rent to anyone with kids because the apartment contained lead paint. Dibari had heard of a law that could require him to undertake major repairs to remove the lead paint. The listing agent did not inform Dibari that he could not legally exclude families with children without violating fair housing laws until she presented an offer to rent the apartment from Sara and Bud. Dibari refused to rent to Sara because of her pregnancy and finally rented the apartment a year later to a single person for $400 per month.

Sara and Bud looked at approximately 30 additional apartments over the next five days, which she later described as "an exhausting, trying, and awful experience." They eventually rented a five-room unit at a monthly rental of $750.

As a result of being denied the subject apartment, Kirschenbaum was shocked, upset, and desperate to find a suitable place in a very short period of time. She filed a complaint with the U.S. Department of Housing and Urban Development alleging violations of the Fair Housing Act based on familial status.

ORDER

INJUNCTIVE RELIEF: ______________________________

____

____

____

COMPENSATORY RELIEF: ______________________________

____

____

CIVIL PENALTIES: ______________________________

____

You Be the Judge

HUD v. Dibari

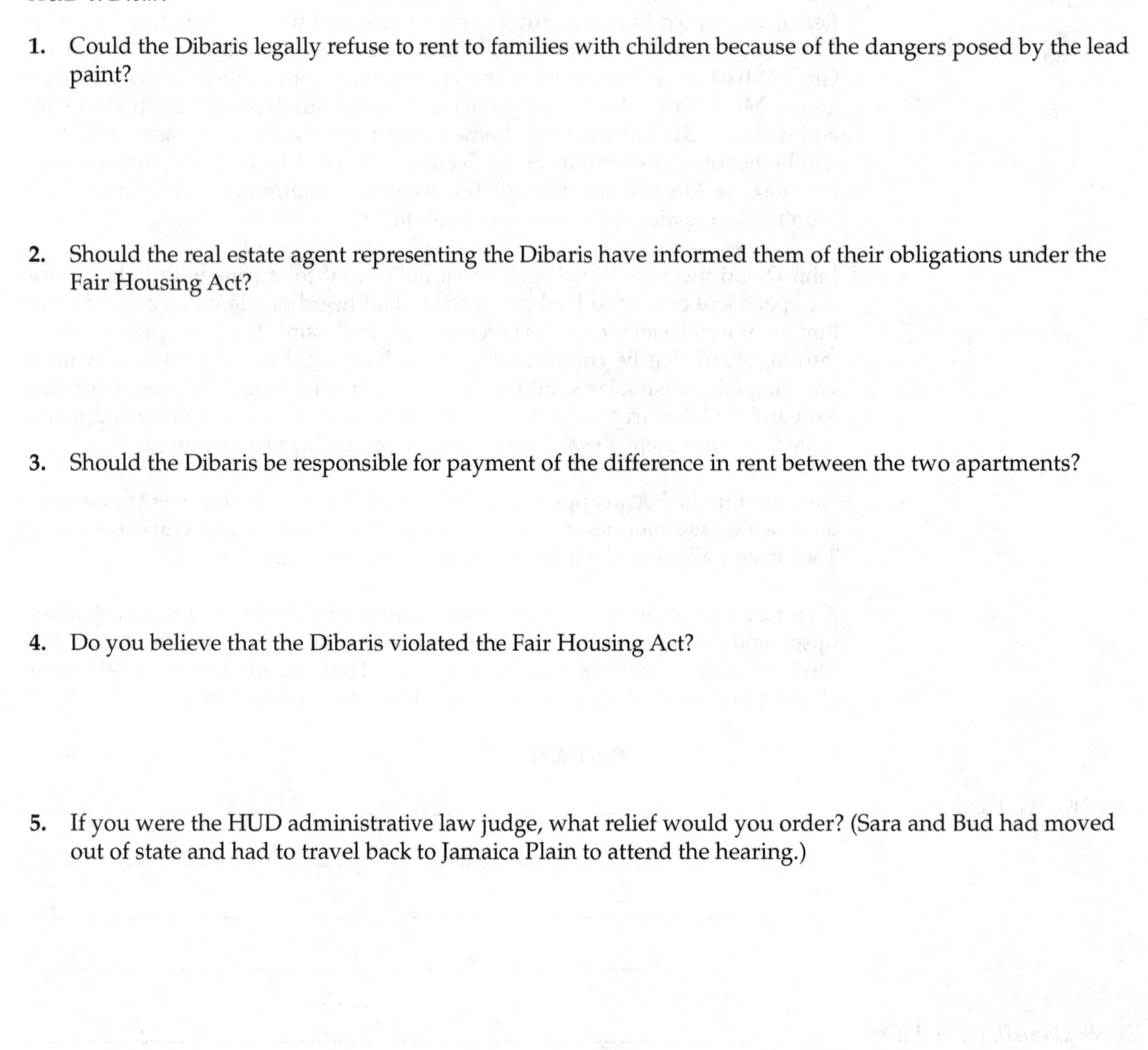

1. Could the Dibaris legally refuse to rent to families with children because of the dangers posed by the lead paint?

2. Should the real estate agent representing the Dibaris have informed them of their obligations under the Fair Housing Act?

3. Should the Dibaris be responsible for payment of the difference in rent between the two apartments?

4. Do you believe that the Dibaris violated the Fair Housing Act?

5. If you were the HUD administrative law judge, what relief would you order? (Sara and Bud had moved out of state and had to travel back to Jamaica Plain to attend the hearing.)

■ *HUD v. Denton*, Waukesha, Wisconsin, No. HUDALJ 059000121

The Westwood apartment complex had a policy of permitting only one child in its two-bedroom apartments because Mr. Denton, the owner, believed that the second bedroom was too small for two children, and further, there were no facilities for a playground. However, the resident manager made an exception to this policy and rented a two-bedroom apartment in March 1987 to the Hoags, even though they had two children, because she thought they would be good tenants.

In November 1987, the Smerlings rented a two-bedroom unit at Westwood. The Smerlings had four children; however, only one child, Mickey, lived with them. Another child, Ishmell, came to live with the family in June 1988. Mr. Smerling operated a maintenance business and soon after moving in began performing maintenance for Denton. The Smerlings breached the terms of the lease on numerous occasions. Mr. Smerling used his master key to the boiler room and replaced his apartment thermostat that limited heat to 70 degrees or less with one permitting heat up to 90 degrees. His son Mickey, who at one time had the master key, terrorized the apartment complex by throwing balls, riding his bike, and running up and down the hallways. Denton concluded that he must take action when Mickey was suspected of starting a fire in the basement of the building.

Denton was hesitant to evict the Smerlings based on the numerous instances of their misconduct because of their working relationship. He was also aware of the new Fair Housing Act that protected families with children from discrimination. He sought assistance from the local housing authority, which he claims told him he had to treat all families of four consistently—that is, if one were to be evicted, all should be evicted. Therefore, in June 1989, Mr. Denton evicted both the Hoags and the Smerlings, citing the occupancy limit which permitted only one child per two-bedroom apartment as the reason.

Both the Hoags and the Smerlings filed a complaint with HUD.

ORDER

INJUNCTIVE RELIEF: ____

____

____

____

COMPENSATORY RELIEF: ____

____

____

CIVIL PENALTIES: ____

You Be the Judge

HUD v. Denton

1. Was Denton's occupancy policy reasonable?

2. Do you feel that both the Hoags and the Smerlings were victims of housing discrimination?

3. Do you believe that the local fair housing authority misinformed Denton concerning his obligations to families?

4. Do you believe that Denton violated the Fair Housing Act?

5. If you were the HUD administrative law judge, what relief would you order?

■ *HUD v. Baumgardner*, Cincinnati, Ohio, No. HUDALJ 028903061

Blanton B. Holley, a single male looking for housing for himself and three male friends, called a telephone number listed on a rental sign at 2343 Victory Parkway. Thomas C. Baumgardner, the owner of 2343 Victory Parkway and about nine other rentals, gave Holley information regarding the monthly rental and estimated utility bills. However, upon learning that Holley and several male friends planned to live there, Baumgardner stated, "I'm not interested in renting to males. My past experience has been that males are messy and unclean." He then indicated to Holley that he had decided to use the house as an office for himself.

Holley contacted HOME, a fair housing organization, to file a complaint. HOME organized several "tests" to determine whether the Victory Parkway home was still available for rent, and whether male and female prospective tenants received equal treatment. A female tester was allowed to view the house for renting to her and other family members. Another female tester later inquired about the property and was told that he was thinking about using the home for an office, but that he would be willing to rent it to her. Soon after, a male tester was told that the house was going to be converted to offices. Later that month, Baumgardner rented the house to a female with children.

Holley, feeling "offended, hurt, insulted, and angered" by the rejection, filed a complaint with HUD alleging discrimination on the basis of sex.

By mistake, HUD sent Baumgardner a housing discrimination complaint about a house in East Chicago, Indiana, and failed to send him a copy of the correct complaint within 10 days. HUD made only minimal efforts at conciliating the complaint and did not complete the investigation within 100 days as required by law.

ORDER

INJUNCTIVE RELIEF: ____________________

____

____

____

COMPENSATORY RELIEF: ____________________

____

____

CIVIL PENALTIES: ____________________

■ You Be the Judge

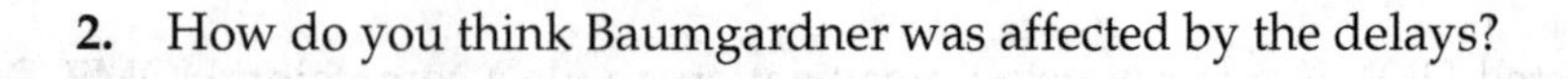

HUD v. Baumgardner

1. Should HUD's procedural noncompliance with the statute serve as a basis for dismissal of the complaint?

2. How do you think Baumgardner was affected by the delays?

3. Do you think Baumgardner violated the Fair Housing Act?

4. Could HOME have conducted the testing more efficiently?

5. If you were the HUD administrative law judge, what relief would you order?

■ *HUD v. Jancik*, Chicago, Illinois, 44 F. 3d 553 7th Cir. 1995

Jancik owned a building in a large housing complex in Chicago. He placed an ad that included the phrase "mature person preferred." Suspecting a fair housing violation, the Leadership Council for Metropolitan Open Communities (the "Council"), a group that promoted fair housing, decided to "test" the property. Gunderson, a white female, spoke with Jancik by phone, and after he learned that she was 36, he stated, "That's good—I don't want any teenagers in there." Jancik asked her national origin, to which she replied, "Norwegian." Jancik asked whether she was "black Norwegian or white Norwegian." Gunderson asked whether he was inquiring as to her race, and he replied affirmatively. They arranged to meet the next day.

Allen, a black female, phoned Jancik two hours later. Jancik asked Allen her occupation, income, age, marital status, race, and whether she had children or pets. Allen did not reveal her race, but did ask Jancik why he needed that information. He stated that he had to screen applicants because the building's tenants were middle-aged and he did not want anyone who made a lot of noise or had children or pets. Allen told him she had no children or pets, and they arranged to meet the next day. Both testers arrived at the building the next day and were told the unit was already rented.

Based on reports filed by the testers, the Council filed a complaint with HUD, alleging violations of advertising rules regarding family status, and violations of interviewing rules regarding race and family status.

ORDER

INJUNCTIVE RELIEF: ______________________________

____

____

____

COMPENSATORY RELIEF: ______________________________

____

____

CIVIL PENALTIES: ______________________________

You Be the Judge

HUD v. Jancik

1. What statements did Jancik make that violated the Fair Housing Act?

2. The advertisement for "mature person" discriminated against what protected class?

3. What discriminatory housing practice did Jancik employ when he told both testers the apartment had already been rented?

4. Did Jancik expressly indicate a racial preference?

5. If you were the HUD administrative law judge, what relief would you order?

final examination a

True/False Questions (Circle the correct answer.)

1. T F The Fair Housing Act of 1968 prohibited discrimination on the basis of race, color, religion, sex, and national origin.

2. T F The 1974 Housing and Community Development Act created the Section 8 housing assistance programs.

3. T F The 1988 Fair Housing Amendments Act called for HUD to implement rules to verify the age of occupants in housing designed for older persons.

4. T F A four-family dwelling unit is always exempt from the Fair Housing Act.

5. T F The practice of steering prohibits housing providers from assigning families with children to ground-floor units for safety reasons.

6. T F States are not allowed to impose more severe penalties for violation of state fair housing laws.

7. T F The Fair Housing Amendments Act of 1988 added handicap and marital status as protected classes.

8. T F The 1968 Fair Housing Act authorized attorney fees awards to only prevailing plaintiffs who were unable to pay.

9. T F FHA lenders are prohibited from considering a person's gender identity in making loans.

10. T F The Equal Credit Opportunity Act includes age and marital status as protected groups.

11. T F Many homeowners' insurance companies contend that the Fair Housing Act does not apply to them.

12. T F A housing provider may inquire whether a person has a disability.

13. T F Covered multifamily dwellings for first occupancy after March 12, 1991, must be accessible to and usable by persons with disabilities.

14. T F The *Hunter* Decision established important judicial guidelines concerning discriminatory advertising.

15. T F The 1995 HUD memorandum concerning advertising prohibits descriptive terms such as *great view* and *walk to bus stop.*

16. T F Housing providers may selectively use human models in advertising without violating the Fair Housing Act.

17. T F The key to composing advertising copy that complies with the Fair Housing Act is to describe the property, not the seller, landlord, neighbors, or "appropriate" buyers or renters.

18. T F An act of discrimination must be intentional for the Fair Housing Act to be violated.

19. T F Evidence collected by testers is not admissible in court.

20. T F An aggrieved person may file a complaint with HUD for two years.

21. T F The statute requires that HUD complete its investigation of a fair housing complaint within 100 days.

22. T F The Department of Justice can assess a civil penalty of up to $50,000 for a first violation.

23. T F Even a small misstep can threaten or destroy relationships with multicultural clients.

24. T F Some cultures have virtually no beliefs that affect the homebuying process.

25. T F In Chinese numerology, the number 4 is considered to be good luck.

True/False Questions (Circle the correct answer.)

1. T F The Civil Rights Act of 1866 is no longer used in housing discrimination lawsuits.
2. T F The 1954 Supreme Court decision of *Brown v. Topeka Board of Education* overturned the "separate but equal" doctrine.
3. T F Refusing to rent a dwelling unit to a convicted drug dealer violates the Fair Housing Act.
4. T F According to HUD, failing to inform any person of desirable features of a dwelling potentially violates the Fair Housing Act.
5. T F According to HUD, there must be a profit before blockbusting activity can occur.
6. T F An appraiser may consider protected class status when estimating the value of property.
7. T F The goal in establishing occupancy standards is to limit the number of children who can live in the property.
8. T F Housing providers are allowed to charge higher security deposits for families with children.
9. T F In developing occupancy standards, a housing provider may consider the number of bedrooms and their dimensions.
10. T F Nothing in the Fair Housing Act requires that a dwelling be made available to an individual whose tenancy would constitute a direct threat to the health and safety of others.
11. T F A building's no-pets policy could be used as a defense for refusing to allow a disabled tenant to have a service animal.
12. T F Alcoholism is considered a disability.
13. T F Housing providers exempt from coverage under the Fair Housing Act are free to employ discriminatory advertising.
14. T F HUD requires that the size of the logotype in display advertising never be smaller than 2 inches by 2 inches.
15. T F Inclusion of information about the availability of accessible housing would violate the Fair Housing Act.
16. T F The wording in real estate advertisements should be reviewed to ensure that no one will feel excluded by what is being said.
17. T F HUD regulations define an "aggrieved person" as including fair housing organizations and testers.
18. T F The disparate impact theory of housing discrimination requires evidence of discriminatory intent.
19. T F Conciliation agreements do *NOT* include awards of monetary damages.

20. T F There are no real advantages to resolving housing discrimination complaints through HUD.

21. T F The maximum civil penalty available in a HUD proceeding is $100,000.

22. T F If a discriminatory housing practice has been found in a business subject to regulation by a government agency, HUD must notify the agency of the final decision and recommend that appropriate action be taken.

23. T F Real estate agents have standing to sue in housing discrimination lawsuits.

24. T F In *Hannah v. Sibcy Cline* REALTORS®, the court ruled that real estate agents have a fiduciary duty to identify the ethnic makeup of a neighborhood.

25. T F Multicultural clients are primarily interested in the quality of the person they choose to represent them.

appendix a

Substantially Equivalent State and Local Fair Housing Laws

Current as of January 2004

States	Localities
Arizona	Phoenix
Arkansas	
California	
Colorado	
Connecticut	
Delaware	
District of Columbia	
Florida	Bradenton
	Hillsborough County
	Lee County
	Jacksonville
	Orlando
	Palm Beach
	Pinellas County
	Tampa
Georgia	
Hawaii	
Illinois	Springfield

States	Localities
Indiana	Elkhart
	Fort Wayne
	Gary
	Hammond
	South Bend
Iowa	Cedar Rapids
	Davenport
	Des Moines
	Dubuque
	Mason City
	Sioux City
	Waterloo
Kansas	Lawrence
	Olathe
	Salina
	Topeka
Kentucky	Lexington
	Louisville
Louisiana	
Maine	
Maryland	
Massachusetts	Boston
	Cambridge
Michigan	
Missouri	Kansas City
Nebraska	Lincoln
	Omaha
New York	Rockland County
North Carolina	Asheville-Buncombe County
	Charlotte-Mecklenburg County
	Greensboro
	New Hanover County
	Orange County
	Winston-Salem
North Dakota	
Ohio	Dayton
	Parma
	Shaker Heights
Oklahoma	
Pennsylvania	Pittsburgh
	Lancaster County
	Reading
	York

States	Localities
Rhode Island	
South Carolina	
Tennessee	Knoxville
Texas	Austin
	Corpus Christi
	Dallas
	Fort Worth
	Garland
Utah	
Vermont	
Virginia	Fairfax County
Washington	King County
	Seattle
	Tacoma
West Virginia	Charleston
	Huntington

Aggrieved person A person who claims to have been injured by a discriminatory housing practice, or a person who believes that a discriminatory housing practice is about to occur.

Bias A preference or preconceived opinion or point of view that does not allow impartiality on anything related to the object, opinion, or point of view.

Catchwords Words that convey that dwellings are available or not available to a particular group of persons because of their membership in a protected class.

Complainant The person who files a fair housing complaint.

Conciliation Attempted resolution of issues raised by a complaint, or the investigation of a complaint, through informal negotiations involving the complainant, the respondent, and the secretary of HUD.

Conciliation agreement A written agreement setting forth the resolution of the issues in conciliation.

Culture The values, beliefs, behaviors, language, and thought processes learned and exhibited by a group.

Discrimination The process by which two stimuli differing in some respect are responded to differently.

Discriminatory housing practice An act that is unlawful under the Fair Housing Act or other fair housing law.

Diversity A description of the uniqueness of each individual; the variety that exists with respect to race, ethnicity, religion, gender, age, familial and marital status, sexual orientation, and physical and mental capabilities.

Dwelling Any building, structure, or portion thereof that is occupied as, or intended to be occupied as, a residence for one or more families, and any vacant land that is offered for sale or lease for the construction or location thereon of any such building, structure, or portion thereof.

Familial status One or more persons younger than 18 being domiciled with a parent or other person having legal custody of such individual; the designee of such parent or other person having legal custody through written permission.

Handicap A physical or mental impairment that substantially limits one or more of an individual's major life activities; a record of such an impairment; being regarded as having such an impairment.

Housing for older persons Housing provided under any state or federal program that the secretary of HUD has determined to be specifically designed and operated to assist elderly persons. Housing intended for and solely occupied by persons 62 years of age and older. Housing intended and operated for occupancy by at least one person 55 years of age or older per unit in at least 80 percent of the units.

HUD Publisher's Notice A notice that publishers should post at the beginning of the real estate advertising section stating that all advertising contained therein is subject to the federal Fair Housing Act, which makes it illegal to advertise any preference, limitation, or discrimination because of race, color, religion, sex, national origin, familial status, or physical or mental handicap.

Major life activities Functions such as caring for one's self, performing manual tasks, walking, seeing, hearing, speaking, breathing, learning, and working.

Multifamily dwelling Dwellings designed to be occupied by more than one family, each living independently of one another.

Ordinary reader Whether or not an advertisement violates the Fair Housing Act will be determined by how an ordinary reader randomly looking at the ad would interpret it.

Protected classes Under the Fair Housing Act, those groups or classes that may not be discriminated against because of their membership in a particular group, or any other groups protected by local or state fair housing laws. The federal Fair Housing Act prohibits discrimination based on race, color, religion, sex, national origin, familial status, and physical or mental handicap.

Prejudice An irrational attitude of hostility directed against an individual, a group, a race, or their supposed characteristics; generally, an adverse opinion formed before sufficient knowledge is obtained.

Punitive damages A damage award aimed at punishing the defendant. Punitive damages are also awarded to deter the defendant and others from engaging in similar conduct in the future.

Reasonable accommodation A requirement under the Fair Housing Act that housing providers make reasonable accommodations in rules, policies, practices, or services when such an accommodation is necessary to afford a handicapped person equal opportunity to use and enjoy a dwelling unit.

Reasonable modification The Fair Housing Act requires that persons with disabilities or handicaps be allowed, at their expense, to make reasonable modifications to the dwelling unit to provide equal opportunity to use and enjoy the dwelling unit.

Redlining The practice of refusing to make loans or otherwise denying financial assistance for housing in particular areas. The term can also refer to insurance companies that discriminate on the basis of the characteristics of a neighborhood where the home is situated.

Rent Includes to lease, to sublease, to let, and otherwise to grant for consideration the right to occupy the premises not owned by the occupant.

Residential real estate–related transaction The making or purchasing of loans, or providing other financial assistance for purchasing, constructing, or improving or maintaining a dwelling, including would-be loans secured by residential real estate; the selling, brokering, or appraising of residential real property.

Respondent The person or other entity accused in a complaint of an unfair housing practice; or any other person or entity identified in the course of an investigation with proper notification.

Steering Attempting to direct members of protected classes toward or away from certain areas or neighborhoods.

Stereotype A fixed, rigid, or exaggerated belief or generalization associated with a category of people.

Chapter 1 Case Study Answers

1. The discriminatory housing practice that occurred in this case study was refusing to sell or rent after an offer, or refusing to negotiate for the sale or rental because of race.
2. Recent HUD decisions have held real estate agents liable for disclosing the race of buyers, even when they terminate listings with sellers who attempt to violate the Fair Housing Act. One such agent was fined $100 and told to take a fair housing class.

Chapter 1 Review Questions Answers

1. b. The Civil Rights Act of 1866 provided equal protection based on race.
2. c. The "separate but equal" doctrine is from the Supreme Court decision in *Plessy v. Ferguson.*
3. d. In *Jones v. Meyer*, the Supreme Court applied the Civil Rights Act of 1866 to both the public and private sectors.
4. c. Sex was added as a protected class in the 1974 Housing and Community Development Act.
5. b. President Lyndon B. Johnson signed the 1968 Fair Housing Act into law.
6. c. An owner must occupy one of the units in a fourplex to be exempt from the Fair Housing Act.
7. c. Showing only currently available property does not violate the Fair Housing Act.
8. c. Showing only properties selected by the prospect does not constitute illegal steering.
9. d. According to HUD, failing to inform a person of desirable features possibly violates the Fair Housing Act.
10. a. The Fair Housing Act does not prohibit a housing provider from refusing to rent an apartment to a convicted drug dealer.

Chapter 2 Case Study Answers

1. Ellis and her family were discriminated against on the basis of familial status. When the law changed in 1988 to protect families with children, Windmill Village should have allowed Ellis and her family to move back in.
2. Yes, Michaels was also a victim of housing discrimination because of the loss of income due to the discriminatory conduct of Windmill Village.
3. This case study is based on an actual case from 1993. The district court held that the housing development discriminated on the basis of family status and assessed a $50,000 civil penalty. The jury awarded $390,500 in damages, with $310,000 of the award going to Michaels for compensatory and punitive damages owing to his business losses.

Chapter 2 Review Questions Answers

1. b. The 1988 Amendments Act made attorney's fees available to prevailing plaintiffs.
2. d. The 1988 Amendments Act added familial status and handicap as protected groups.
3. c. College students are not a protected class.
4. b. In *Hill v. Community of Damien of Molokai*, the Court ruled that enforcement of restrictive covenants would violate the Fair Housing Act.
5. d. Predatory lenders have targeted minorities and elderly women.
6. a. The ECOA covers applications for mortgages and is not enforced through HUD.
7. c. In *City of Edmonds v. Oxford House*, the Supreme Court ruled that a group home's location must be reasonable and necessary to accommodate disabled residents.
8. d. The definition of handicap does not include current illegal drug users.
9. a. HUD has declared that volunteering information regarding a current or former occupant's disease of AIDS is illegal.
10. a. The Americans with Disabilities Act does not cover housing.

Chapter 3 Case Study Answers

1. Yes, a discriminatory act occurred here. Housing providers are not allowed to consider risks and circumstances of a dwelling when making rental decisions. Therefore, this was an act of discrimination, refusing to rent based on familial status.
2. No. Health and safety concerns may not be the basis for refusing to rent to a family with children.
3. Yes, the Daltons would have been exempt from the Fair Housing Act if they had not hired a leasing agent to represent them.
4. If the Daltons had rented out their home by themselves and used a discriminatory ad stating "No Children," they would have lost their exemption because of discriminatory advertising.

Chapter 3 Review Questions Answers

1. b. Running a credit check on an applicant does not violate the Fair Housing Act.
2. c. A landlord's health and safety rules cannot be overly restrictive toward families with children.
3. b. Participation in the Section 8 program is voluntary.
4. c. A property manager may charge, on a case-by-case basis, a deposit to restore the unit after a modification is made.
5. c. In developing occupancy standards, a landlord may not consider the lack of playground facilities.
6. b. Occupancy standards exist to prevent overcrowding. The *Oxford House* decision stated that occupancy standards are not for the purpose of preserving the family character of a neighborhood.
7. c. A landlord may not consider whether an adult and a child will share a bedroom in developing occupancy policies.
8. d. The definition of handicap does not include current illegal drug users.
9. b. The Fair Housing Act does not allow a landlord to ask an applicant about the nature or severity of a disability.
10. c. The Fair Housing Act allows a landlord to require that a resident pay money over a reasonable period of time to restore the dwelling after modifications are made.

Chapter 4 Case Study Answers

1. Yes, the Fair Housing Act applies to publishers of telephone books.
2. The publisher could establish a policy that whoever sells the advertising is responsible for making sure that all ads comply with the Fair Housing Act before they are approved for publication.
3. The publisher of the telephone book agreed to pay $25,000 for the all-adult ad in the yellow pages.

Chapter 4 Review Questions Answers

1. b. A housing provider exempt from the Fair Housing Act may not place an ad indicating no children.
2. d. The *Hunter* opinion established that the Fair Housing Act does apply to newspapers and other media and that applying the Act to newspapers does not violate the First Amendment guarantee of freedom of the press.
3. c. An advertisement containing the phrase "accessible units available" does not violate the Fair Housing Act.
4. b. The case stating that human models must reasonably represent both majority and minority groups in the metropolitan area was *Spann v. Colonial Village*.
5. d. The 1995 HUD memorandum does not prohibit the terms *master bedroom* or *bachelor apartment*.
6. d. The key to composing advertising that complies with the Fair Housing Act is to describe the property.
7. b. Newspapers that publish the HUD Publisher's Notice may still be sued for violations of the Fair Housing Act.
8. b. According to HUD, the term master bedroom does not violate either the race or sex discrimination provisions of the Act.
9. b. Seemingly harmless words may trigger a complaint under the Act.
10. d. The term *fisherperson's paradise* in an ad would least likely violate the Act.

Chapter 5 Case Study Answers

1. It really did not make any sense for Lepieux to remove this case to federal district court.
2. No, the damage award would not have been as great with HUD because no punitive damages are available through HUD. This case study is based on an actual case where the defendant eventually had to file bankruptcy after the lawsuit was over.

Chapter 5 Review Questions Answers

1. b. An aggrieved party does not need to file a complaint with HUD before filing in federal district court.
2. c. Plaintiffs who have standing to sue include testers and persons who are current residents in a cooperative association.
3. d. One advantage of filing a direct court action is the availability of punitive damages.
4. b. Aggrieved persons may file a complaint with HUD for up to one year.
5. d. HUD must complete its investigation of a fair housing complaint within 100 days.
6. b. The disparate impact theory requires no evidence of discriminatory intent.
7. b. It is the disparate impact theory, not the disparate treatment theory, that provides the means of holding housing providers liable for the results of their conduct.

8. c. The maximum civil penalty that an ADJ may impose is $65,000 and is used in situations where two or more violations have occurred within a seven-year period.
9. d. The maximum civil penalty available in a lawsuit by the Justice Department is $100,000 and is used in second-offense situations.
10. c. The statute of limitations for a fair housing discrimination lawsuit in federal district court is two years.

Chapter 6 Case Study Answers

1. Yes, Dylan Realty probably violated the Fair Housing Act by referring the Lee family to the only Asian real estate agent in the company. If the Lee family had made the request for an Asian agent, that would be different. There is not a lot of case law that would support this answer, but we know that people may not be treated differently based on race.
2. Yes, Wong did indeed steer her clients to specific neighborhoods based on race. She did not show all available housing or offer a variety of choices because she decided for them that they should locate in a predominantly Asian neighborhood.
3. If the Lee family wanted to limit the housing search based on their race, Wong could have directed them to organizations that could have identified suitable neighborhoods for them, and they then could have informed Wong of these areas.

Chapter 6 Review Questions Answers

1. b. Valuing diversity is quite important when working with multicultural clients.
2. b. In the United States, maintaining steady eye contact indicates sincerity and interest. Avoiding eye contact is a sign of respect in some cultures.
3. c. People from Germany and Australia are typically very prompt.
4. b. People from "negotiating" countries often try to keep negotiating even after the purchase agreement is signed.
5. a. The color red in feng shui denotes fire and is said to bring fame and fortune.
6. b. The court ruling in *Zuch v. Hussey* stated that real estate agents may never influence a customer's housing choice on racial grounds even in response to a buyer's initiative.
7. b. Having a death occur in a property is not always a significant issue for people.
8. b. The Fair Housing Act does not permit assigning people of the same culture to a particular section of a building.
9. d. The court in *Hannah v. Sibcy Cline REALTORS®* ruled that real estate agents do not have a fiduciary duty to be the source of the information, or the source of the source of the information, regarding the racial or ethnic makeup of a neighborhood.
10. b. The Fair Housing Act does not prohibit a person from marketing real estate services to any particular culture or group.

Chapter 7 Case Study Answers

HUD v. Blackwell

1. What discriminatory housing practice would you cite in this case study?

   To refuse to sell after the making of a bona fide offer, or to refuse to negotiate for the sale, or to otherwise make unavailable or deny a dwelling because of race.

2. Could Wainwright join in the lawsuit against Blackwell?

   Yes, real estate agents have standing to sue in housing discrimination lawsuits.

3. How was Blackwell protected by the decision to have the case determined by HUD administrative law judge?

   There are no punitive damages available in a HUD proceeding. This case was particularly egregious, and a federal district court may well have awarded a large punitive damage award.

4. Were the Coopers victims of housing discrimination?

   Absolutely. They had to change the locks and move out, and they feared for their personal safety.

ORDER:

INJUNCTIVE RELIEF:	Blackwell was ordered to honor the sale and was prohibited from damaging the property. He was enjoined from future discrimination against the Herrons or anyone else because of race.
COMPENSATORY RELIEF:	Herrons—$44,590 Coopers—$20,595
CIVIL PENALTIES:	HUD—$10,000

HUD v. Dibari

1. Could the Dibaris legally refuse to rent to families with children because of the dangers posed by the lead paint?

   No. Excluding families with children from dwellings because of dangers posed by lead paint violated the Fair Housing Act based on discrimination based on familial status.

2. Should the real estate agent representing the Dibaris have informed them of their obligations under the Fair Housing Act?

   Yes. At the time the Dibaris indicated they would exclude families with children, the agent should have spoken up and informed them of their obligation under the Fair Housing Act not to discriminate against families with children.

3. Should the Dibaris be responsible for payment of the difference in rent between the two apartments?

   No. Sara K. and her husband selected a larger apartment.

4. Do you believe the Dibaris violated the Fair Housing Act?

   Yes. Families with children may not be excluded from housing based on safety reasons.

ORDER:

INJUNCTIVE RELIEF: Injunction against future discrimination against Sara K. or anyone else based on familial status. HUD supervision for three years.

COMPENSATORY RELIEF: $200 for inconvenience
$200 for emotional distress

CIVIL PENALTIES: $200 to HUD

HUD v. Denton

1. Was Denton's occupancy policy reasonable?

   No. Housing providers are not allowed to limit the number of children. Also, he arbitrarily decided that the second bedroom was too small for more than one child.

2. Do you feel that both the Hoags and the Smerlings were victims of housing discrimination?

   Yes; however, HUD did not award any damages to the Smerlings. Denton should have evicted the Smerlings based solely on the repeated lease violations, not based on his occupancy standards.

3. Do you believe that the local fair housing authority misinformed Denton concerning his obligations to families?

   Probably not. Denton may have misunderstood what he was told regarding families with children.

4. Do you believe that Denton violated the Fair Housing Act?

   Yes. His occupancy policy discriminated against families with children.

ORDER:

INJUNCTIVE RELIEF:	Injunction against future discrimination against the Hoags or anyone else based on familial status.
COMPENSATORY RELIEF:	Hoags—$3,000 for inconvenience; $10,000 for emotional distress; $210 out of pocket
CIVIL PENALTIES:	HUD—$2,000

HUD v. Baumgardner

1. Should HUD's procedural noncompliance with the statute serve as a basis for dismissal of the complaint?

   No. That would have unfairly punished the complainant in this case.

2. How do you think Baumgardner was affected by the delays?

   He did not keep written records of events and conversations, so he had to rely on memory to re-create the facts and circumstances. Obviously the delays made his defense to the charges more difficult.

3. Do you think Baumgardner violated the Fair Housing Act?

   Yes. He discriminated based on sex. He misrepresented the availability of the dwelling by indicating through words or conduct that a dwelling available for inspection, sale, or rental had been sold or rented.

4. Could HOME have conducted the testing more efficiently?

   No. The testing produced the intended results, which showed that Baumgardner treated male and female testers differently because of their sex.

ORDER:

INJUNCTIVE RELIEF: Injunction against future discrimination against Holley or anyone else based on sex. HUD supervision for two years.

COMPENSATORY RELIEF: $2,000 for economic loss (reduced to $1,000 on appeal)
$500 for emotional distress (affirmed)

CIVIL PENALTIES: $4,000 to HUD (reduced to $2,000 on appeal)

HUD v. Jancik

1. What statements did Jancik make that violated the Fair Housing Act?

   "That's good, I don't want any teenagers in there." He asked whether a tester was "black Norwegian or white Norwegian" after he had asked about her national origin. He also responded affirmatively when asked whether he was inquiring into her race.

2. The advertisement for "mature person" discriminated against what protected class?

   Familial status.

3. What discriminatory housing practice did Jancik employ when he told both testers the apartment had already been rented?

   Discriminatory representations on the availability of a dwelling—indicating through words or conduct that a dwelling that is available for inspection, sale, or rental has been sold or rented.

4. Did Jancik expressly indicate a racial preference?

   No, Jancik did not expressly indicate a racial preference, but the context of Jancik's racial questions indicated an intent to discriminate.

ORDER:

INJUNCTIVE RELIEF: Injunction against future discrimination against anyone based on race or familial status. Refrain from using advertising that discriminates against families with children.

COMPENSATORY RELIEF: Leadership Council—$21,386
Marsha Allen—$2,000
Attorney's fees—$23,842

CIVIL PENALTIES: HUD—$10,000